# INTO THE LIGHT

## Half-Century as Missionaries in Brazil

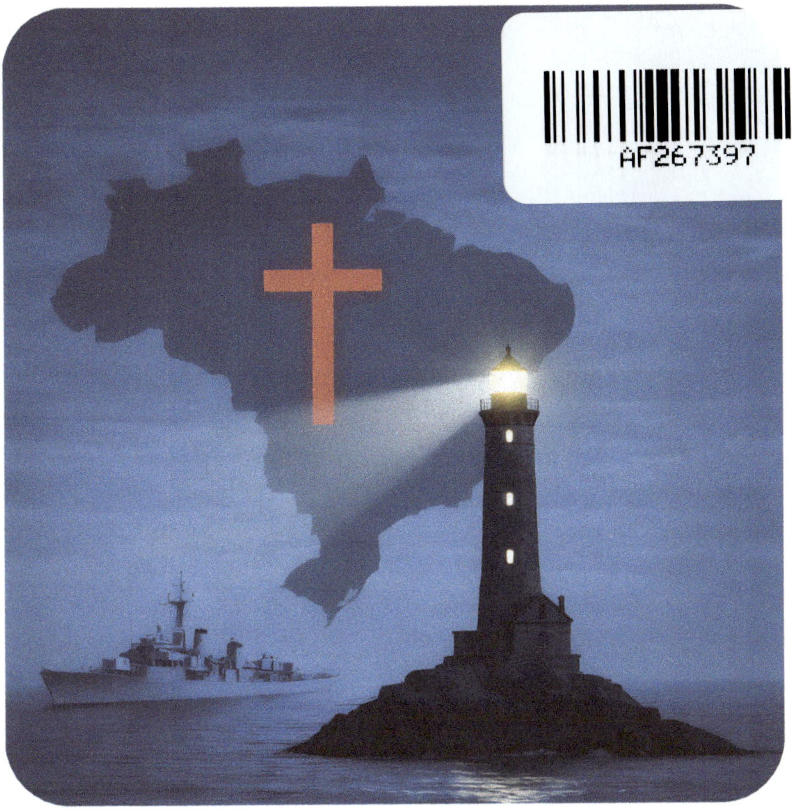

## Dr. Tom Latham

DynoTech Publishing, Colorado Springs, Colorado, USA

Edited and published by Dave Carlson, DynoTech Publishing, Colorado Springs, Colorado, USA. (www.dynotech.com)

This book may be ordered through booksellers or from IngramSpark.

ISBN: 978-1-885708-18-2 (paperback)

Scripture quotations are from the King James Version (KJV) of the Bible.

Library of Congress Control Number: 2025927400

Print information is available on the last page.

Printing History:
        February 2026:        First Edition.

# Contents

# DEDICATION

This book is dedicated to Missionary Penny Sue Latham, who gave her life to serving her Lord first and her family second. The Lathams were blessed beyond measure with her generosity and creative spirit. The art she left behind will always remind us of her God-given talent and her dedication to knowing Jesus and making him known to everyone who crossed her path.

*EXAMPLE OF PENNY'S BEAUTIFULLY CREATIVE ARTWORK*

# FORWARD by Mike Whitesell

Tom and Penny are the quintessential missionary couple. Their mutual respect and devotion to Christ led them to love, serve, and proclaim their faith to the people of Brazil. Tom is continuing that decades-long calling with astonishing vitality and passion.

Tom is one of the most interesting and compassionate followers of Jesus I have ever met. His unique life story and his friendship have together challenged and encouraged me to be a better man, husband, and servant of Christ.

You're getting ready to read an exhilarating account of the story about two people who were, in Tom Latham's own words, "crazy in love with Jesus and willing to serve Him anywhere in the world." In God's providence, Tom and Penny ended up in Brazil. What an adventure it has been!

From a difficult childhood few of us can imagine, to a transformative encounter with Christ, Tom was immediately launched into a life of education, evangelism, and church planting with Penny, the love of his life.

Prepare to read about dramatic conversions, innovative ministry approaches, multiple robberies, opposition faced inside and outside the church, and touching, redeeming relationships that developed over the years.

The Latham family stayed in our home several times over the years. They regaled us with some of these stories, treated us to Tom's famous cinnamon rolls, and shared his sense of humor. Their story of serving our Savior is unique in every way.

Having passed the age of eighty, Tom continues his ministry. After reaching 100 years, he intends to be recognized by the *Guinness Book of World Records* as the 'oldest youth pastor/ wrestling coach in the world.' Read this book. You'll have little doubt that it could happen.

**Mike Whitesell, Former Pastor,
Community Church, Battle Creek, Michigan**

*Mike and Kathy Whitesell were always a blessing to us.*

# AUTHOR COMMENTS

*Into the Light* describes what happened to me as an abandoned adolescent who developed into a troubled teenager. I was floundering around, pleasing only myself. On May 6, 1964, as a troubled young man, I was faced with the eternal penalty for the lifestyle I had chosen.

Deciding to accept the offer of salvation by grace alone, I jumped out of the darkness surrounding me and ran to 'The Light of the World' (John 8:12). Jesus accepted my sinner's prayer of repentance and salvation, giving me eternal life, as He promised to anyone who would call on Him.

Storytelling is one of my passions, and through my books, I strive to convey joy, invite reflection on my faith, and move readers emotionally through real-life experiences. If my stories move you emotionally, I have succeeded.

Some images and illustrations in this book were generated or enhanced using artificial intelligence (AI) technology to enrich your reading experience.

Dr. Tom Latham

God only had one Son and He made Him a missionary.

**Here are some kind words from a few of my many dear friends:**

*It has been a delight to know and follow the life and ministry of Dr. Tom Latham for 55 years. He is a faithful and fruitful servant of God. If I were still teaching my course, 'Lives of Great Missionaries,' I would make this autobiography a required reading.*

> *Dr. Sam Telloyan, former missions teacher*
> *at Pillsbury Baptist Bible College*
> *in Owatonna, Minnesota*

*It has been a joy to get to know Tom and Penny Latham over the past 17 years. I saw their heart for the Lord and His people reflected in their small acts of kindness and in their help with developing and mentoring young lives.*

> *Mike Martin, South American Field Director,*
> *Baptist World Mission*

*My fellowship with the Lathams began fifty years ago when I was the leader of the South American Prayer Band at Pillsbury Baptist Bible College. Both churches I pastored supported the Lathams, with the last one being their sending church. God has blessed their lifetime of faithful service, to which I gladly give witness.*

> *Dave White, former pastor, Bryant Avenue Baptist*
> *Church, Minneapolis, Minnesota*

Your updates are the most encouraging thing you do for those who pray for you around the world. I think your ministry has been worldwide for all these years, and I am glad and blessed to be part of it. Your impact is huge. It resembles your heart and has allowed me to 'learn to serve so I can serve to learn.'

Douglas Hazewinkel, former Pillsbury College wrestler, National Champion, 1976

Tom lived a crazy, adventurous life in his early years. The option was there for him to have been voted the most unlikely to succeed in life! BUT Tom knew when he got saved, he wanted to be a preacher. Many of us back then did not have a clear direction for our lives, but Tom did! I continue to marvel at how he allows God to use him in so many ways, places, and times! This book is packed with examples of what passion looks like in the life of an energetic believer.

Richard L. Bilyeu General Building Contractor (retired), Redmond, OR

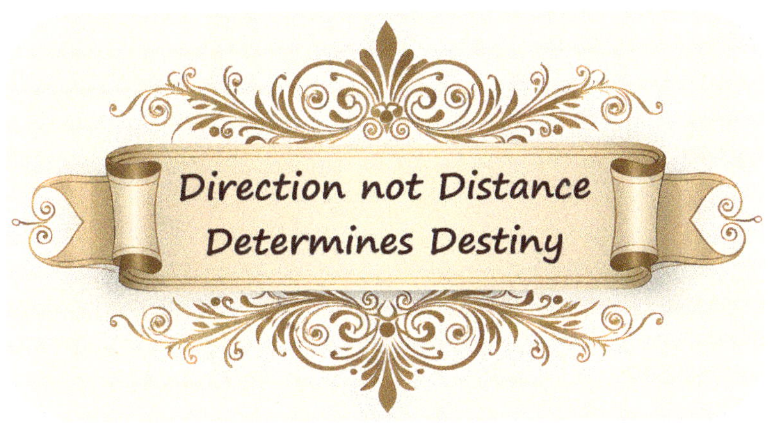
Direction not Distance
Determines Destiny

TOMMY (AGE 2) AND HARRIET (AGE 4)
[ME AND MY SISTER]

# CHAPTER 1

# Who Coulda Thunk It?

On March 7, 1945, at a small hospital in Lebanon, Oregon, Loretta Elvira Latham gave birth to her second child: ME. I weighed just four pounds and six ounces. World War II was drawing to a close, but the government still stamped my birth certificate, allowing our family to buy one extra pound of red meat.

After my birth, Mom—Loretta Latham—took me from the hospital to Grandpa John Franklin Taylor's farm beside Crabtree Creek, near the small town of Lacomb, Oregon. There, the town's entering and leaving signs stood on the same post above a population sign that now boasted 151 residents, counting me.

We stayed at the farm for a month. Then, my parents, Harry and Loretta, took my sister Harriet and me to visit family in Newark, Ohio. When we returned to the farm ten months later, I weighed less than 10 pounds. That was worrying.

The doctor who delivered me told Grandma Ella Mae, Grandpa's second wife, "Every time Tommy opens his mouth, put something in it or he won't make it."

Grandma fed me with an eye dropper, and if you could see me now, you'd know how well that worked! Harriet and I stayed on the farm until I was two years old, under the loving care of Grandma Ella and Grandpa Jack. Everyone in the family called her Grandma Shortie because she was so close to the ground, or as they say nowadays, 'vertically challenged.'

*Kosy (front) and me enjoyed our visit with Grandma Shortie.*

Mom came back for us, and Grandma protested. "Jack, if you let Letty take the kids, I'm leaving you. They came here almost dead, and I saved their lives." Grandpa always had a soft spot in his heart for his only daughter. That was probably because his first wife abandoned the family when Mom was only nine years old, leaving her to do the housework and cooking, without the marvelous Cinderella ending. Grandma Shortie left.

With Harry Latham gone, and Danny Boucher now my half-brother, instability became our normal. We moved constantly, relying on the bare minimum, and spent months in boarding homes. Alcohol cast a long shadow, defining much of our family's struggle.

Danny was two years younger than me. Harriet and I tried to calm his tormented soul when he cried out for his mother late at night in various boarding homes.

I atenderd several schools in the San Francisco Bay Area. At the end of my second grade, we made some moves toward Oregon. I remember seeing the gun used in the robbery Mom was involved in, which sent her to the California Institute for Women in Chino. She spent three years there for theft and passing bad checks.

Harriet, Danny, and I ended up back on Grandpa's farm. Julia was Grandpa's third wife. She was a great lady who enjoyed hunting white-tailed deer and catching rainbow trout. Because Grandpa already had four mouths to feed, we saw Danny shipped off to his French-Canadian father in Washington State.

Grandpa told Harriet and me, "If you want any school clothes, you'll have to work in the fields all summer." We left home at 6:30 AM and worked all day in the fields. We had our lunch in a brown paper sack. During the next three summers, we worked picking strawberries, raspberries, blackcaps, cherries, boysenberries, plums, bush beans, and pole beans. We also picked wild blackberries, which we sold.

After working long days, we enjoyed splashing in Crabtree Creek. With our modest earnings, we shopped for school clothes at Polly Potter's Trailer—shirts cost a dime and worn jeans a quarter. Halfway through the fifth grade, Mom was released from prison. She took us to Lebanon, Oregon, and Danny rejoined us.

We sometimes did things that would get parents in trouble today. For example, the three of us left at dusk, walked through the fields behind our house, and ended up below the drive-in theater screen. We snuck into the Kuhn Drive-In, watched a movie at a speaker, and returned home around midnight. Today, it's hard to imagine parents letting kids do this.

I had a daily paper route for the *Oregonian*. I would deliver papers across town—two trips on Sundays.

Right after Mom married Robert Parsons, Bobby came into the family. We eventually moved to Hopland, California. 'Bud,' as our stepfather was called, worked in the lumber industry.

After finishing grammar school in Hopland, I prepared to start high school. The summers were blazing hot; I often flipped my pillow to cool off. That summer, Mom left us for good, moving across town and leaving me to care for Danny and Bobby. Harriet married and moved out, though she still lived nearby.

Alcohol remained at the center of our family's troubles. My mom's struggle with addiction brought constant upheaval and pain, shaping our futures in ways that became impossible to ignore.

Our neighbor friend invited Danny and me to trash a house he said his dad was going to tear down anyway. We broke out the windows, threw homemade spears through the walls, and flooded the floor. Three days later, a policeman asked to see my tennis shoe. It matched the pattern left on a pile of sheet rock at the house. We should have realized the pile of sheet rock was a sign they weren't going to destroy the house, but fix it. We were just dumb kids.

Dad had to take Danny and me to see the judge in Ukiah, California. Because I had to take care of Danny and Bobby while Dad worked, the judge fined us just $100 and let us go. This was my first run-in with the law. Danny was shipped back to his father.

I started high school with a stepfather and a stepmother, Ruby. She was an excellent cook and a marvelous person. Her daughter, Gayle, and son, Jerry, also lived with us.

In my first year, I played on the junior varsity basketball and baseball teams. During this time, I was walking down the road when a local police officer stopped and told me to get into the car. "Tommy, you're in big trouble; you and your friends were smoking in Tom Asher's trailer and burned it down."

*I am #20 (front right) on this junior varsity basketball team.*

"What? I don't smoke, and none of my friends do, either." Well, that got me off the hook for something I didn't do.

One night at a school dance, I 'borrowed' Robert Hiatt's Lambretta scooter. It started without a key. I took off with it. Since I didn't know how to drive the scooter, it turned over. When I picked it up, and attempted to drive again, it went straight into a tree. Robert came out and saw his bent steering fork.

I told him I was not stealing the scooter, just using it. I also told him I would pay to repair the damage. He said, "Was the scooter yours? NO! Did you take it without permission? YES! That's what good people call stealing."

He called the law, and the law picked me up. I was taken home and put in the custody of my stepfather, Bud. The police officer came to the high school the following Monday and got me out of class. I was taken to the juvenile holding facility in Ukiah and spent the night in solitary confinement. My stepfather came the next day and got me out of jail.

After finishing my first year of high school, I made the biggest mistake of my life. Mom offered to give me half of a 1948 Ford if I would come and live with her. Most of the time when she wanted me to be with her, it was because of the welfare checks. I fell for it, breaking Bud's heart.

Later that year, the same police officer picked me up again and said, "Tommy, you're in real trouble now. I have an eyewitness who says he saw you coming around the fire station, carrying a gas can. You stole gas out of the fire engine. How awful! What kind of a person are you, anyway?"

I told him I didn't do that. "We have an eyewitness," he said. "Are you saying it was not you?" I told him I was there, but I wasn't carrying a gas can. He believed me and didn't ask me what I was holding. It was a six-pack of beer, which is about the same size as a small gas can.

At this point, trouble escalated for me. My path mirrored the chaos of my family life—stealing liquor and lacking guidance. Each step seemed to confirm that turmoil was my inheritance.

During the summer, I had a job hauling hay. Since I had to give my half of the '48 Ford to my stepbrother, Mom arranged for the purchase of a 1951 Chevy convertible. She used my money to pay $75, leaving a debt of $150, to be paid later. I was elated to now have my OWN car.

One day, when I came home from hauling hay I noticed all of Mom's dresses were cut up, lying on the bed. I knew her current husband did it. Not wanting to confront him, I looked for Mom at the tavern where she worked. She had gotten her wages and left town. I was abandoned again!

With nowhere to turn but Grandpa's farm, I hurried back home to pack a few things in the '51 Chevy. Then, I headed out of town. Survival and searching for belonging were constants I lugged around with me.

Leaving California, I got to Medford, Oregon, at 6:30 AM. The police stopped me because I was a teenager driving a car with an out-of-state license plate, so early in the morning. I was a short kid who could barely see over the steering wheel.

The car was registered in the name of Loretta Clark, not Latham. I only had a library card, not a driver's license. They accused me of stealing the car. I asked to make a phone call. They didn't let me make the call. I insisted. "I've watched enough Perry Mason to know I'm allowed to make one phone call."

They laughed at me as they slammed the steel door with an authoritative clank. I was in jail for a week. No one in my family knew I was there—no one! I finally wrote a letter to Grandpa. The counselor read it and asked to see me.

"What's the matter, Tommy? Don't you like it here?"

Surprised by his question, I replied, "To be honest, Sir, there are a thousand places I'd rather be. What I did deserves a fifteen-dollar fine, not a week in jail." He found Grandpa's phone number and called him.

Grandpa came to get me the next day. He was furious with the police, and I thought I heard him say the word 'suing.'

We got the Chevy and went home. I told Grandpa I was going to work in the fields during the summer, but then I was returning to Hopland. He said I was not going back: "You're going to stay here and finish high school." So, I worked in the fields and stayed.

*I found refuge several times with my grandfather, John F. Taylor, and his wife Julia at their farm in Lacomb, Oregon.*

*Grandpa was the only man who had a positive influence on me throughout my adolescence. He was also a fervent protector of his family.*

*Julia was a great fisher-woman and hunter of the white-tailed deer. Her cooking was fabulous, especially her waffles, pancakes, bread, and chocolate nothing cake.*

# CHAPTER 2

## Bullies

Almost everyone has met a bully at some point in their life. Since I've become a follower of the Nazarene, I handle bullying situations differently. The following three examples happened before I became a Christian.

**Bully Example #1**

Dale Spelbring was a teenage neighbor in Hopland, California. Dale I went to my grandfather's farm in Lacomb, Oregon, the summer before I started at Hopland High School. We planned to make some extra money by working in the fields.

One Saturday afternoon, we were hitchhiking to my Aunt Carol's house. A car with six teens passed us, and someone yelled, "Pull in your thumb; we're going to give you a ride."

Since I had attended five grammar schools in Lebanon, I recognized the kids in the car. Knowing their reputation as smart alecks and bullies, I suspected they would drive us twenty miles away and leave us stranded—a common trick. I was determined not to fall for it.

They came back, pulled up alongside us, and someone yelled, "We told you to pull in your thumbs, and we'd give you a ride. Now, get in."

I was adamant, "We're not getting in the car so you can take us twenty miles and drop us off."

They piled out of the car and told me I was a smart aleck, and now I had to fight one of them. I said, "I don't want to fight anyone."

They told me I had to fight someone, or they were going to beat both of us to a pulp. I didn't see any way out of this predicament except to fight one of them. "Okay, I'll fight Dick Potts, since he's my size."

"No, you won't," Dick said. "You're going to fight Bart Hudson."

Bart was the biggest of the group. I still didn't want to fight, but I couldn't outrun them with Dale there. I said, "Okay, but I don't want to get blood on my nice shirt. Let's take our shirts off."

They agreed. I quickly took off my shirt, and as Bart was pulling his shirt over his head, I rammed my head into his stomach, knocking him against the car door handle. I started to punch him in the nose.

He held up his hand, saying, "Don't be picking on a cripple now." It was then I felt the metal brace from his left knee to his shoe. I didn't know he had a brace.

"This was your idea in the first place," I said. "Don't complain now that you lost." For some reason, Dale and I were then given a ride all the way to my aunt's house.

**Bully Example #2**

By my senior year, I already believed that bullies will continue their behavior if no one stands up to them. When walking down the school hall with my neighbor friend, Tom Rutherford, I was suddenly punched by the school's toughest kid, who was accompanied by his friend.

I had never picked on anyone or started fights, so this unprovoked attack was especially concerning. If I didn't react, he would likely keep picking on me. Bullies act this way. As he came walking by me again, I pushed his friend into him, knocking the bully into the lockers.

Now the real fight began. He threw me to the floor, sending my pens flying all over the place. He was on top of me and about to punch out my lights. I yelled, "Stop! If we fight inside the school building, we'll both be expelled. Let's take this fight outside."

A crowd gathered to watch the scene. Knowing the bell would ring soon, I slowly picked up my pens to delay the fight. He grew impatient: "Hurry up! I want enough time outside to beat you to a pulp."

"Take it easy! Take it easy! I have to get my pens." It was evident I was stalling. To give me an incentive to speed up, he pushed me. Finally, I had no excuse. I got up and started slowly walking to the door.

He didn't like that, so he pushed me again. "Get moving, or I won't have time to pulverize you!"

Just then, the school bell rang. I looked him in the eye and said, "I'm not getting a tardy slip so you can fight me. I'll see you later." I hurried to my next class, relieved he fell for my tactic. He never bothered me again, which was the result I wanted.

## Bully Example #3

The third story took place at a movie theater with three Rutherford boys. While we were in the lobby, Bill Larkin—who was a foot taller than me—grabbed my shirt collar and pulled me close. "I don't like your ugly look. I want to rearrange it," he threatened.

I grabbed his shirt and pulled him down nose to nose with me. "I don't like being threatened."

"You're not going to escape," Bill retorted. "I'll follow you at school and harass you until we settle this."

Not wanting trouble at school, I suggested, "Let's go to the parking lot and settle this now." We went near my car and swung haymakers at each other, but neither of us landed a blow.

Suddenly, a police car pulled into the lot. "HEY! What's going on here?" one of the police officers hollered.

We put our elbows on the hood of my car and pretended to arm wrestle. When they saw this, they left, thinking it was nothing. After this, we both went our separate ways. As I said before, I never started fights and never wanted to be in one.

## On a Lighter Note

This story demonstrates that a creative solution can turn a challenge into an opportunity. My cousin, Lee Moore, Tom Rutherford, and I faced a dead car battery in town. Because two of us were unable to push the car fast enough to get it started, we tried flagging down other teens for help, but none stopped.

I had an idea, "You know how teens will gather to watch a fight?" I asked. "Let's fake a fight and maybe a car full of teens will stop to watch us fighting and will give us a push."

My cousin and I began throwing punches that missed. The first car of teens stopped when they saw us. When they realized what we were up to, they thought our plan was clever, and helped us start the car.

> *"For God so loved the world, that He gave His only begotten Son, that whosoever believeth in Him should not perish, but have everlasting life."*
>
> *John 3:16*

*MY SISTER (HARRIET), BROTHER (DANNY), AND MOM*

*I graduated from Lebanon Union High School in 1963. I was the first person in my family to graduate from high school.*

# CHAPTER 3

## Grace and Grace Alone

I started my junior year at Lebanon Union High School. Since I had attended five different grammar schools in the area, I recognized many classmates. To keep gas in my '54 Chevy—bought for thirty-five dollars—I worked various odd jobs. In the spring, I tried out for the baseball team but was cut from the roster.

Work defined my early years: from chopping and delivering firewood for Uncle Bunky to moving irrigation pipes on a bean farm between school years. I couldn't find steady work during the year. In the fall, I pursued wrestling. After losing a close wrestle-off by one point, I was cut from the team.

That spring, two friends and I traveled to Hood River to plant trees for the forestry service. While there, we shoplifted and, after stealing gas while drunk, we were arrested. Grandpa got me out of jail again. Grandma Julia gave me a stern lecture, which I deserved.

Since my grandfather and two uncles were sailors, I joined the Navy Reserve and went to a monthly meeting on Friday night.

Upon high school graduation, I was supposed to take the most dangerous job in the woods: putting the cable on a felled tree so the caterpillar could pull it out of the ravine. If the cable ever breaks, the 'choke setter' had better be faster than the descending log, or he was a goner. I had the tools and steel-toed shoes, ready to start on Monday.

On Sunday night, the logging company supervisor called. The job I expected was given to a school-bus acquaintance. I was upset and left without work. I chose to enlist in active duty with the Navy. Three months later, the cable broke on that logging job, killing my friend. That could have been me!

After seven weeks of boot camp in San Diego, California, I attended the Electrician's Mate school on the same base. After graduating, I was assigned to the USS Interceptor AGR-8, a radar picket ship out of San Francisco. The ship went out to sea for five-week tours, 500 miles off the West Coast. Our job was to make sure no airplane came into United States airspace without identifying itself, or it would be shot down.

*As a Navy electrician, I made it to third-class petty officer before finishing one year of active duty.*

My first assignment on the ship was working in the scullery, washing dishes. I was about to find out why I used to get carsick on Oregon's winding roads. I had an inner ear problem that caused me to get extremely dizzy and nauseous. This is why I would throw up on the rides at the Strawberry Fair.

The ship's rocking back and forth was a serious problem for me. I was washing dishes and puking into a bucket when Richard Edwards, a weatherman, stuck his head in the scullery. He said I looked terrible, and green—like The Hulk. When I told him I was seasick, he said he had the same problem. He offered to pray for me.

Whenever I needed advice, I went to Richard, who invited me to attend Calvary Baptist Church in San Francisco. Because Richard had duty, I went to the church by myself on May 6, 1964. After the church service, a teenager named Marie Liedecker asked me, "Sailor, do you know where you're going to go when you die?"

"Yes, and it's not a pleasant thought."

That night, Wayne Buford, another sailor, drove me to Aunt Cleo's house across the bay. A student from Western Baptist Bible College was also sitting in the front seat. He explained the simple plan of salvation. Learning about 'grace alone' marked a spiritual turning point for me.

When we stopped under the streetlight in front of my aunt's house, I prayed a simple prayer of salvation. I asked the Lord to forgive my sins and come into my heart and save me from hell. After I prayed, I raised my head and said, "This is great. I'm going to be a preacher." That was a prophecy!

After going into my aunt's house, I tried to explain to her what had just happened to me. She didn't get it, but she did give me my first Bible—a *Scofield Reference Bible*! Most of the men on Aunt Cleo's side of the family were professional wrestlers and criminals. Her husband was in prison.

Her eleven-year-old son, Mike, allowed me to spend the night in his bedroom. I asked him if he wanted to go to hell when he died. He said he did not. "Well, if you want to go to heaven, you have to do what I just did: confess your sins to God and ask Jesus to come into your heart and save you."

He said he wanted to do that. We prayed together. Though I had been a Christian for only an hour and didn't know any Bible verses, I had already shared what I received—grace and grace alone.

When I got back to the ship, I changed my clothes and went to work in our office, not saying anything to anyone. After a bit, one of the sailors said, "Hey, Latham, what's going on?"

"What's your problem?" I asked.

"Well, you've been working here for twenty minutes and haven't cussed once or told a nasty joke; what's going on?"

My silence was a testimony, of sorts. "Last night I accepted Jesus Christ as my Savior." The cat was out of the bag, for sure. Because I told them I was going to church to check out all the good-looking girls, they laughed at my conversion story.

I had already planned to attend the Saturday night dance in Hopland with my old classmates. The town was only one hundred miles north of the Bay Area. I caught a Greyhound bus to Hopland.

I went to the event, but didn't dance. As I sat there, the Holy Spirit spoke to me, "Tom, this is not your crowd anymore. You know what's going on here and what will happen after the dance.

I have better plans for you. Don't ever come back to a place like this."

I had only been saved for three days and hadn't had much time to read the Bible. Still, I sensed a strong pull from the Holy Spirit and never returned to a place like that.

Soon, the ship's captain asked for someone to lead the *Protestant Divine Services* while we were out to sea. My friend Richard and I volunteered. The captain accepted our offer. I'd lead songs, and Richard would preach; the following Sunday, we changed places.

I volunteered to say the morning prayer while we were out to sea. Later, the Captain asked to see me. He said I was preaching more than praying. He was also concerned about my using the name Jesus, because it might offend a Jewish person. I assured him there was not one Jewish person on our ship. I had checked that out. He told me to quit preaching and start praying. "This is your first and last warning."

When I would go to the bridge to offer a prayer, a certain quartermaster consistently harassed me with filthy language. He also switched the microphone off and on while I was praying, so my voice would break up on the ship's speaker system. Richard told me about the quartermaster's actions.

My following prayer was, "Lord, if anyone has Jesus as his Savior, he is a child of yours. Jesus said, 'Whoso shall offend one of these little ones which believe in me, it were better for him that a millstone were hanged about his neck, and that he were drowned in the depth of the sea.' (*Matthew 18:6*)" We were 500 miles off the coast of Washington State.

When I left the bridge, the Captain met me, pointed his finger in my face, and said, "Latham, I warned you. You just lost your praying privileges."

Reflecting on my journey as a new Christian, I realized blending zeal with knowledge was key. While I made mistakes, holding onto my early enthusiasm and growing through experience became my guiding principle. The coming years would show how this combination shaped my life.

*CALVARY BAPTIST CHURCH*
*SAN FRANCISCO, CALIFORNIA*

# CHAPTER 4

## Shore Duty

*Dr. Roy Austin baptized me and was my first mentor when I was a new Christian. He was 92 years old and living in South Dakota when he came to hear me speak at a supporting church. This was the first time he ever heard me preach.*

While serving as a sailor, I joined the youth group at Calvary Baptist Church in San Francisco. After being baptized by Pastor Dr. Roy Austin a few weeks into my faith, I felt eager to serve and asked to help in the church's teaching ministry.

He said, "Tom, you've only been saved for a few weeks. Give it more time."

I often wanted to be in control, though I didn't realize it stemmed from my choleric personality. I asked, "How much more time?"

"Come back in a month or so and then talk to me."

In thirty days, I was back, "Well, here I am again."

"I was speaking figuratively, Tom. Give it more time," he replied.

When the youth group went tobogganing at Lake Tahoe, I was off duty and able to join them. As I left the ship, Richard, stuck on quarterdeck duty, called, "Latham, break a leg."

I had never been on a toboggan before, so I chose the front seat. We sped down the hill, hit a ridge, and crashed. At first, I laughed, but then I felt a sharp pain in my left leg. Both bones in my lower leg were broken.

My friends rushed me to a small hospital. After X-rays and pain medication, the doctor set my leg. While groggy, I began sharing my faith with him and even gave him a gospel tract.

Richard felt bad when I returned to the ship with a cast up to my hip. When I hobbled up the gangplank, he said, "I was just kidding. You know that, right?"

The yeoman (secretary) told me to hurry down to the ship's office, because they had orders for me to get off the ship before it pulled out for a five-week tour off the coast of Mexico.

My pastor, Dr. Roy Austin, had called the ship's captain and asked, "Are you planning on taking Tom Latham out to sea?"

"Yes, we are."

"Do you have a doctor on board?"

"No, we don't."

"Do you have an X-ray machine on board?"

"No, we don't."

"Well, I don't think it's a good idea to take him out to sea, where he has to climb steep ladders to get anywhere, especially off the ship. If he fell into the water, how would that work for him, with a full-leg cast? He'd sink like lead."

The captain was immovable, "He'll be okay. Don't worry about him. We'll put him in the engine room on a chair so he can watch the electrical panel all day long."

Dr. Austin was the pastor every sailor needed. "I'm getting the drift you don't see my point," Austin said. "Okay, I'm going to call the *San Francisco Examiner* and tell them this story."

When I returned from shore leave they had new orders for me to get off the ship as quickly as possible for duty on land. Because I was a petty officer, I was put in charge of a transit barracks on Treasure Island Naval Base, where our ship was docked. This assignment would last for five weeks.

At roll call one day, I recognized a sailor from boot camp—a rough drinker, like I once was. Not wanting to interact, I quickly took roll and turned away. He shouted, "Hey, Latham, is that really you?" I responded reluctantly, but he was pleasant. I invited him to church, and he was saved on his first visit. I realized God often used me to win souls—sometimes unwillingly.

I traded my full cast for a walking cast up to my knee. While I was walking on a street in downtown San Francisco, a man came toward me. We were the only two on the sidewalk. He had a cast on his left leg, just like I did. After he passed me, we turned around and gawked at each other. We hobbled toward one another and began chatting.

I invited him to church. He showed up drunk. I had to hide him in the coat closet until the service was over. By that time, he had sobered up enough to accept Christ.

I made a deal with the Lord. "Anytime You want to break a leg or an arm for someone to be saved, You have my permission." (As if the Lord even needed it!)

When food came to the docks, all sailors, third class and below, had to be a part of the 'grocery convoy.' They brought supplies aboard, carrying the goods on their shoulders. The last time they did this it went well, until they brought the watermelons aboard.

It appeared the Navy had bought one hundred melons, but only eighty got to the cooler, below deck. This time, they advised us petty officers would be stationed at key points to ensure all the melons reached the locker.

One sailor in our unit justified sneaking away with a melon. "What difference does it make if we eat it in the dining hall or here? It's our melon, and we can eat it anywhere we want. I'm going to grab one for us."

Because I had only been saved a short time and used to be a skilled thief, I accepted the other sailor's logic and secretly hid a melon. Later, when he bragged about his trick, using the word 'stole,' I reconsider and wanted nothing to do with it.

At midnight, I returned to the scene of the crime, grabbed the melon, and quietly sneaked into the kitchen. Unfortunately, the cook had arrived early to make cinnamon rolls. He looked at me and smirked, "Aha! That's where one of our melons went!"

Apologizing, I told him I was returning the melon. If this info could be kept just between the two of us, I'd appreciate it. He was a wise and compassionate man. He told me to hightail it out of there before anyone else came along.

Through this experience, I learned to hold firm to my biblical convictions, resisting worldly reasoning that could lead me back to old habits.

Among my Navy activities, I also organized a wrestling tournament for my shipmates. Since only a few sailors were interested, I devised three categories: lightweight, middleweight, and heavyweight. I was a lightweight, but entered the middleweight division so others wouldn't think I had organized the tournament just so I could win a trophy.

I was pinning all my opponents in less than a minute. A sailor approached me and asked, "Would you like to make ten dollars?"

"How?" I responded, wondering where this was going.

He told me he bet Jones he could last more than a minute against me and offered half the winnings if I let him. It felt dishonest, like something from the Maritime Mafia!

Back when I was an unsaved sailor, I probably would have accepted his offer. The situation had now changed significantly. Not agreeing to his offer, I just walked away. I pinned him in thirty-five seconds. He said, "You just lost ten dollars."

As I helped him up, I replied, "Right, but you just lost the match." This is the only trophy I ever won, and it's still in my office at church.

Another memory I have from my Navy days was my romantic interests. Marie Liedecker was the first girl I dated after becoming a Christian. She broke up with me because I wouldn't 'make out' with her. I was now a Spirit-controlled sailor with different priorities. The second girl I dated broke up with me because I kissed her on the cheek. I really didn't know where to go or what to do after that!

Shortly after getting saved, I heard that George Kochian, a deacon in the church, had bunk beds in his basement. He let sailors stay there when they didn't have to be aboard the ship. I asked him if I could be one of those sailors. He told me to come on over and be part of his family.

He charged us ten dollars a week. This didn't cover the electricity for Richard to take his forty-minute hot showers, nor the three-story sandwiches I made. What a wonderful person George Kochian was!

J.R. Shucfulsky was a sailor on another picket ship. He wasn't a Christian but stayed at George's house now and then. We were in a public pool one day, and he showed up with liquor on his breath. I asked him where he had been. He said he was teaching a religion class at his church.

I thought this was interesting. We started discussing the differences between his liturgical church and our conservative, Bible-believing church. After a while, he began to stroke his wet chin. He started thinking. When I asked him to consider salvation by grace, he said he would.

He became a Christian, joined our church, went to Bible college, and got married. With his family, he became a missionary to Haiti. Of the five sailors who stayed in George's basement, two became missionaries, and two became pastors, showing how spiritual growth and support can bear fruit.

# CHAPTER 5

# Experience in Evangelism

I was bold in my witness as a sailor. One evening, while an officer was doing paperwork in an office, I was typing a summary of what each book of the Bible taught. I turned my chair and inquired, "Sir, can I ask you a personal question?"

It seemed my approach was already known among the 125 men on our ship. Without looking up, the officer said, "Latham, I know what you're going to ask. I'm a Christian, but I do like to smoke a cigar now and then. And I take a swig sometimes. That'll be the end of our conversation." That was the end of it.

When satellites came into use, our ship no longer needed to monitor the West Coast. All eighteen ships on both coasts were being decommissioned. I was scheduled to leave the Navy in a few weeks, just before our ship was retired and put in mothballs.

Our last service on the ship was held on the Sunday before we reached San Francisco. By that time, services took place in the library. Only one sailor, Dan Gardner, came. I asked whether he still wanted the service. He said he did. My friend Richard, who usually helped with services, was on duty. I waited a bit for more sailors, then closed and locked the hatch.

I questioned whether it was worthwhile to hold a full service for just a single sailor. I realized it gave him the rare chance to focus entirely on the message, free from others' opinions or distractions. After delivering my sermon, I said, "You've been attending our services for quite a while. I believe you know how to be saved." Then, I asked him, "Would you like to kneel here right now and accept Christ as your Savior?"

Not hesitating, Dan got on his knees and started praying. That's the only service on the ship where we had any decision-making.

Later, after leaving the Navy, I went with our youth group to attended an area meeting. Dan was there. He said, "Latham, I really did accept Christ as my Savior that day on the ship. Thanks for making it happen."

*I bought my brother Bobby a Navy outfit in 1965.*

# CHAPTER 6

# A Civilian Again

In June 1965, my active duty service ended, and I entered the active reserve. One weekend a month, I served on the USS Twining DD-540 at Treasure Island in the Bay Area, reporting Friday night and leaving Sunday afternoon.

COLORIZED PHOTO OF USS TWINING DD-540

During this period, I bought a '54 Chevy but couldn't afford the $900 annual insurance. To manage costs, I sold the Chevy and purchased a 1965 Honda Dream, a 150cc motorcycle, for $500—insurance was only thirty-five dollars a year. After getting the bike, I rode to Oregon to visit my grandparents, who had moved from their farm to Newport, on the coast.

While I was in Oregon, news arrived that my cousin Lonnie Moore had been killed in Vietnam. When I was in the sixth grade, I spent a lot of time with his family, since they lived nearby. Later, I visited the Vietnam War Memorial in Washington, DC, and did a pencil rubbing of his name, now displayed in my church office.

Back in San Francisco, a church member helped me find a job at her husband's restaurant, Manning's. I first washed dishes for several weeks, then moved to their location at the Kaiser Building in downtown Oakland, where I served coffee and washed dishes.

I always worked quickly and also did a good job. Dishwashing took others three hours; I finished in two. Using my spare time, I cleaned the large, messy ovens, even though they were still warm.

When the cook came the next morning, he asked, "Who cleaned the ovens?" No one knew, so he figured I did it. "Why did you do that?" the cook asked.

"I had some spare time."

"I've never seen any workers do anything more than they were required to do," he said.

I left there with a letter of high recommendation.

I was my family's first high-school graduate. By starting my first semester at Western Baptist Bible College (WBBC) in El Cerrito, California, I also became the first college attendee in my family. This milestone came about because of the change in my life after Jesus saved me.

I was nominated for freshman class president but didn't win. When the school needed a volunteer leader for Saturday afternoon street evangelism in downtown Oakland, I stepped up and took the role.

Each Saturday, our team left campus around 4:00 PM and spent an hour speaking with people in the area. On average, we led 5–10 people to Christ each week. I had my team prepare stamped postcards with their addresses for new converts, so they could contact us. We sent them follow-up materials and information on churches near their homes.

I got a job at a laundromat, where I watched over the place during business hours and cleaned up after closing. I made friends with kids who stopped by, and eventually started an afternoon Joy Club in the back, near my desk. Dr. Austin later gave me a junior Sunday school class. Kevin Ames, a student of mine, is the only one still there from my time at the church.

During Christmas break, I stayed on campus because I worked close by. I was alone in the dormitory. Money was scarce, since I paid my own school bills. For several days, I ate only a few cans of black olives and started losing weight, which I didn't need to lose.

That spring, I joined the baseball team. Even though I lacked skill, I made the team because few students wanted to play. Many of them skipped daily practice, but I attended every session because I loved the game.

One day at practice, only Coach Jim Huckeby and I showed up, so we just threw the ball around. At season's end, Coach joked, "If we had a trophy for faithfulness, Tom Latham would get it." Although there was no such trophy, I played enough innings to earn my first varsity letter and was now considered an athlete.

Ironically, I was cut from a high school baseball team, yet I made a college team!

*PILLSBURY BAPTIST BIBLE COLLEGE (PBBC)*
*"OLD MAIN" ADMINISTRATION BUILDING*
*OWATONNA, MINNESOTA*

*PBBC closed in 2008. Since April 2014,*
*the campus has been called Camp Pillsbury.*

*Photo courtesy of the U.S. Library of Congress*
*Carol M. Highsmith's America Project (2019).*

# CHAPTER 7

## California Youth Pastor

I was on the Western Baptist Bible College (WBBC) Missions Team. We went to various churches on Sunday night to give testimonies and sing. I usually told my life story and played the harmonica.

At the end of the spring semester, the school informed me I would not be able to take the finals because I still owed $300 on my bill.

I called Grandma Julia and asked her to have her mother, a devout Christian, pray for me regarding my financial need. We went to a Baptist church in Monterey, California, where Grandma Julia's brother came to hear me play my harmonica. Afterward, he asked if it was true I needed three hundred dollars to pay my bill, so I could take my finals. When I confirmed, he took out his checkbook and wrote a check for the full amount. This was the first time someone helped with my school bill. Grateful to God for this provision, I was able to take my final exams.

I enjoyed going to WBBC. Someone, however, told me about a Bible college in Owatonna, Minnesota, that had a wrestling team.

I looked into it, and decided to attend Pillsbury Baptist Bible College (PBBC). I was going to drive my Honda motorcycle there after leaving WBBC. Before I left, I learned the government was extending the GI bill to anyone who had served in the military during the Vietnam War, which had started in 1958.

This was good news for me. It would cost only $900 a year to attend PBBC for room, board, and tuition. The government said it would send me $125 a month. Finally, someone was going to help me with my school bill—my rich Uncle Sam!

Since I didn't need to work all summer to pay next year's school bill, I decided to accept an offer to serve as the summer youth pastor at First Baptist Church in Avenel, California, in the desert area of the Kettleman Hills.

During the summer, I organized activities for the teens and gave rides on my Honda. I would take teenage boys to the top of a hill, where I shared my faith. On the day before my last planned movie activity, I was washing my bike and noticed a young man cleaning his car. I invited him to that night's church movie.

He smirked at me. "You're the guy giving rides to teens and telling them they would have to walk down the mountain if they didn't accept Christ as their Savior."

"What are you talking about?" I asked. He told me he had heard I was giving boys a ride to try to force them into making a religious decision, or they would have to walk home.

Surprised, I explained what really happened: "I could've worked all summer for money, but I chose to spend my time taking boys for rides and sharing with them how they could be saved by accepting Jesus as their Savior. Now you share this accusation, which offends me greatly."

He backed off and apologized. He came to the meeting that

night, saw the film, and became a follower of Jesus. To our knowledge, that was the only decision for the whole summer's work.

After my summer ministry, I had to go on a two-week underway training cruise with my Navy ship. Our ship left port in San Francisco and docked in San Diego. In addition to visiting the famous San Diego Zoo, I attended Scott Memorial Baptist Church, where Tim LaHaye was pastor.

After my Navy training cruise, I returned to Treasure Island to retrieve my Honda. When I arrived, I found an MP about to ticket and tow the bike. Thankfully, the MP was Dino, a friend from the USS Interceptor. Pleased to see me, he tore up the ticket. I believed the timing was providential and gave him a gospel tract.

George Kochian bought me a sleeping bag and handed me his credit card, telling me to put all my expenses on it. After spending the night, I left for Oregon early the next morning to visit my grandparents. I stopped in Hopland, California, and stayed with some friends, sharing my testimony of salvation and some Chick tracts.

I had planned to spend a day or two in Oregon visiting relatives before leaving for PBBC in Minnesota. Unexpectedly, my cousin Andrew Newburg, whom I had looked after, was killed by a speeding car. I stayed for his funeral. Our family was heartbroken by the loss of this wonderful boy, just eleven years old.

This put me a bit behind schedule for getting to PBBC in time for registration. Early the next morning, I was off to Minnesota.

Me with my 1965, 150cc Honda Dream, which I rode from San Francisco, California to Owatonna, Minnesota to attend Pillsbury Baptist Bible College.

# CHAPTER 8

## MINUS 70 Degrees is NOT Acceptable

My trip's timing couldn't have been worse. At midnight, I found myself at 11,000 feet—about twice Denver's elevation—with cows blocking the road. I could not eat or sleep until I got down the mountain. I finally reached a city at 3:00 AM. There, I parked my bike on the grass at the park in the town center. For security, I tied my motorcycle wheel to my foot, crawled into my sleeping bag, and got two hours of rest.

You might be asking yourself, "Why didn't Tom use George's credit card to get a motel room?" Okay, I didn't want to take advantage of his kindness. Besides that, I had only planned to sleep for a few hours and hit the road again. If I didn't hurry, I'd miss registration. I never liked being late for anything.

Halfway across Montana, my bike's engine started missing. I stopped, removed the spark plug, and discovered a piece of carbon closing the gap and shorting it out. Using my pocketknife, I cleared the carbon, replaced the plug, and got back on the road.

I pushed myself to the limit: nineteen hours of driving on the first day, twenty-one on the second, and twenty-two on the third, to make it to Owatonna. When I finally arrived at 3:00 AM, the night guard let me sleep in the dorm on an empty bunk.

With no extra clothes—just what was on my back—I registered

for classes the next day. Even Dr. Cedarholm, the College president, noticed and asked if jeans and cowboy boots were all I owned.

"Sir," I said, "my clothes are being shipped to me. They should arrive any day now."

"I hope so, Son," was his kind reply.

My first job in Owatonna was as a janitor at McKinley Elementary School. I rode my bike to work until it became too cold. Then, I stored my motorcycle in Dr. Richard Weeks's garage, a faculty member, and waited for spring before riding again.

Starting wrestling season at 150 pounds, I knew I wasn't good enough to compete with Dan Lindsey at 145 or Bob Bardwell at 137. If I wanted to make varsity, my only chance was to lose weight and challenge for the 130-pound spot. I knew I did not have the experience to win any matches above 145 pounds.

The challenge was that Jay Braccini, the team's toughest wrestler, held the 130-pound spot. Even to challenge him, I needed to lose twenty pounds. During wrestling season, I skipped the dining hall and ate a dozen scrambled eggs daily, cooked at the snack bar. I stocked up on chocolate bars and kept fruit juices cold outside my window.

My break came when Jay had to step down for a semester. My new goal was to beat Dennis Hinds and Dave Leslie to get the varsity spot. I did that and was on the team!

In my first college match, I was pinned by Dale Hartle from Owatonna High School, who was wrestling for Rochester Junior College in Rochester, Minnesota. I pinned my next ten opponents. Every year I won the 'MOST PINS' award, since I wanted to get off the mat as soon as possible.

Besides working for the public school, I also had the job of clearing the ice and snow from the sidewalk between the dining hall and the dormitories at PBBC. The night guard would wake me up at 5:00 AM to chip ice and shovel snow. This was no job for a California sunshine dude.

Freezing! No hat, jacket, or gloves could keep the biting north wind of the frozen tundra from hurting my eyes. I literally had ice growing on my eyelashes.

My goal was to find Christian work. However, with 700 students majoring in Bible needing Christian service each week, all Sunday school classes were filled. Street evangelism was out of the question, with temperatures dropping to forty below zero and wind chills making it feel like seventy below.

Several of the girls I dated eventually broke off our relationship. Before wrestling practice began, I was in a serious relationship; I considered her my fiancée, and was supposed to meet her parents during Christmas break.

At the last chapel service before Christmas break, someone passed me a note. It read, "Tom, it's not going to work for us. I'm not going to take you to see my parents. Have a Merry Christmas." I was shocked—this was no way to break up with your fiancé, and I was heartbroken.

A friend gave me a ride to Des Moines, Iowa, where I started hitchhiking to California. My idea was to stay at George's place and find some holiday work. Hitchhiking was a bad idea in the middle of winter. I was freezing on the highway. At midnight, a car pulled to the shoulder of the road. If I had not jumped into the ditch, it would have killed me.

Finally, at 2:00 AM, I got a ride with a rock band. They took me to Lincoln, Nebraska. I called George from the Greyhound Bus Station. He sent me fifty dollars to buy a ticket to California. Over school break, I worked for a friend of George's, delivering televisions in the Bay Area.

I wasn't able to find Christian work in Minnesota, struggled with the cold, and was feeling lost after my fiancée ended things. Determined to find my place, I decided to transfer back to WBBC after my semester ended at PBBC.

George arranged for me to purchase the church's 1960 Volkswagen bus. The night before I was to leave the Bay Area, I placed my contact lens case on the nightstand. When I woke up, it was nowhere to be found. The only logical explanation was that a pack rat had hauled it away.

I couldn't wait to get new contacts, so I drove the bus to Minnesota without glasses. My vision was 20/100, which was very bad. I had the choice of staying in San Francisco to have new contacts made or driving without them so I wouldn't miss my final exams.

George gave me his credit card again for all my expenses. Just before crossing into Nevada, I passed a teenager hitchhiking. Turning around, I offered him a ride. Before we got to the mountains of Montana, he accepted Christ.

This trip was rough. In Wells, Montana, I stopped to rest, but it was so cold my thin sleeping bag didn't keep me warm. I decided to drive, but the motor wouldn't start—it didn't want to leave California either. I eventually got a tow truck to give me a jump start.

There were times when I had to get out of the VW bus and walk close to the road sign to read it. This was a nightmare of a trip, ending in a snowstorm fifty miles from Owatonna. I was determined to take finals, though, and drive the bus back to San Francisco.

During finals, things changed unexpectedly for the better: Pastor Virgil Fitch visited, searching for a youth pastor. Noticing my Navy background and connecting because of his own Army service, he chose me for the position. I finally found the Christian work I was seeking and decided to stay in Minnesota.

*I'm relaxing on the couch with my life-long friend and retired Navy weatherman, Pastor Richard Edwards.*

SHANE AND PENNY AT HIS ORDINATION

# CHAPTER 9

## Great Minnesota Squirrel Test

With the end of wrestling season still two months away, I began my job as a youth pastor. This meant my ministry at First Baptist Church of Spring Valley competed with my need to maintain wrestling weight. Mrs. Fitch, the pastor's wife, was an excellent cook, but I couldn't eat her meals. Every weekend, the Main family, farmers in the church, gave me six dozen eggs to take back to school, which greatly helped my wrestling diet.

My primary responsibilities at church included:

- *Organizing a youth activity every other Saturday.*
- *Teaching the teen boys' Sunday school class.*
- *Leading a youth meeting each Sunday at 6:00 PM, before the evening service began.*

Erma Werth, one of our church members, was a wonderful, kind, and spiritual woman who loved people. She taught a Sunday school class for junior girls until she was too old to get to church.

Despite harsh Minnesota winters, Erma was determined to get her four children to church. Deep snow often made it impossible to get the car out of the driveway, and at times, the motor wouldn't start in -50° wind chills.

Vernon, her son, went to Pillsbury with me. I talked him into wrestling in a Pillsbury tournament so we wouldn't have to forfeit five points for a weight class. That was the end of Vernon's wrestling experience as a skinny 123-pounder.

The Werths were down-to-earth, like my grandpa and grandma in Oregon, who took me in to live with them several times. The Werth family liked to hunt deer, ducks, and squirrels—yes, squirrels!

One Saturday night, I arrived for dinner, and Erma greeted me with a smile. "We have a special treat for you, Tom," she announced. Knowing Erma, I suspected a surprise. At the table, she set down a large plate of golden fried, skinny-looking critters. "Amil was lucky this week to find some squirrels. Have some!" she said, watching for my reaction.

For someone who was raised on clams, clam chowder, clam pancakes, rainbow trout, and all kinds of white-tailed deer dishes, this fried squirrel looked interesting. I dove into the freshly-cooked critters and expressed my gratitude, as well as my heartfelt compliments to the chef.

I later learned this was their way of testing newcomers: could you eat squirrel meat without reacting? I passed by eating heartily, earning my place as an accepted Minnesota hillbilly.

Pastor Fitch later invited another young man from California to serve as music leader and my assistant. He drove a 1966 Trans Am from San Jose, California to Owatonna. We took turns driving to church events—me in my VW bus one weekend, him in his Trans Am the next. I secretly preferred his car over mine!

When the weather warmed up, my assistant told me he was

going downtown to pass out gospel tracts. I stayed at church to study. Pastor Fitch caught me. "Tom, do you know where your assistant is?"

"Yes, he's downtown passing out tracts."

"No, he isn't! He's outside of town, drag racing with the locals. Are you telling me you don't know anything about this?" Pastor Fitch asked.

"Right! I didn't know this," I replied.

That was the end of the Trans Am coming to Spring Valley. I asked Pastor Fitch to consider my roommate, Bill Terrey, as the music leader. Pastor Fitch interviewed him, and Bill got the job.

The Pillsbury wrestling team was good. The first four weights were almost a sure win, as was the heavyweight wrestler, Chuck Woods. We had a student coach, Bill Kettlewell, who wrestled at 175 pounds. We won the conference title, and I won the 'most pins' award.

A month before school ended, a recruiter came to campus seeking students to sell a dictionary for five dollars each. He promised significant earnings for a ten-week summer stint, which appealed to me, so I signed up.

I got a book. It took me only ten minutes to sell it in Owatonna. This summer plan would have helped me because I wouldn't have to work during the school year. I could just wrestle and study.

As I was coming back from selling the book and walking up the stairs to Pillsbury Hall, Steve Cornelius, my good friend, was at my side. I looked at him and said, "Steve, I just sold one of those dictionaries in ten minutes. I'm going to spend the summer making lots of money, so I won't have to work during the school year."

Steve said, "That's great if it's the will of God."

Why did he have to say that? I was going to make a lot of money. I prayed about it and decided not to make a drastic decision based only on money. I decided to be a camp counselor all summer and that's where I met Penny. If I would have sold the dictionaries, I wouldn't have met her.

*Amil and Erma Werth hosted both Penny and me while we worked with the teens in Spring Valley.*

# CHAPTER 10

## George Kochian

Of all the people God brought into my young Christian life, George Kochian was the most influential. He was a deacon at Calvary Baptist Church in San Francisco, California, and lived at 307 Baltimore Way.

*George Kochian wasn't my dad, but like my grandpa, he was a father I never had.*

After learning that George welcomed sailors to stay in his basement, I asked if I could be included. He greeted me warmly, saying I was free to come by. Whenever liberty allowed me off the ship, I spent my time at his house, relaxing, eating, tanning, and exploring San Francisco on George's Lambretta 125cc scooter.

Lillian, George's wife, was an excellent cook, and she often made Sunday noon meals that became the highlight of the week for sailors. George also trusted me with his VW bus, allowing me to drive teens from Calvary Baptist Church to different places around the Bay Area.

George was a steady support, a spiritual compass, and an insightful counselor. He taught biology at a public school, keeping piranhas, tarantulas, and snakes in glass aquariums at home. Eventually, he became the principal of the school serving military personnel on the Bay Area Treasure Island Naval Base.

Here are some of the things George did for me:

- *Loaned me money to buy the church's VW van;*
- *Gave me his credit card twice to pay travel expenses;*
- *Gave me a Pen-F 35mm camera to take photos on my trip to the Holy Land, Greece, and Rome;*
- *Came to my ordination in 1973;*
- *Came to my graduation when I got my doctor's degree;*
- *Came, with his wife, to visit us in Brazil;*
- *Loaned us money to build the foundation of our house;*
- *Asked friends not to buy flowers for his funeral, but to send the money to us in Brazil; and*
- *Supported us with a monthly gift of $150.*

After Lillian passed away, George married Lois. She became an excellent partner and firm supporter. Lois has continued the monthly support for my ministry, even since George's passing.

George's generosity and genuine care for many sailors, whom he called 'his boys,' demonstrated how one dedicated person can impact lives by living out their faith and investing in others.

For me, George became like the father I never had, and he

enjoyed being called 'Papa.' He always treated me kindly and offered sound advice. His guidance kept me on track until I could make sound decisions on my own.

Whenever I needed anything, George never hesitated to help. The world needs more people like him—selfless mentors who make a lasting difference.

> *"Let nothing be done through strife or vainglory; but in lowliness of mind let each esteem other better than themselves. Look not every man on his own things, but every man also on the things of others."*
>
> Philippians 2:3-4

*MY 1969 TRIP TO EGYPT*

**www.campchetek.org**

*Camp Chetek is a fundamental Baptist ministry located in Chetek, Wisconsin, on the southwest corner of Lake Chetek. The camp's legacy dates back to Pastor Ralph Berry, who in 1925 held a youth Bible camp at a Boy Scout camp near its current location. Despite a rocky history, the Camp coalesced in the 1960s during its expansion.*

*1967 VW BEETLE*

# CHAPTER 11

# Camp Chetek

After school ended, I drove my VW bus to California with some students, who helped pay for the trip. Unfortunately, someone had set my motor valves at .004 mm instead of .008 mm. By the time I reached San Francisco, the motor was already scorched.

Driving back to Owatonna, I spotted a VW dealer in Rapid City, South Dakota, and decided to stop. I asked what they would give me for my bus toward a new 1967 VW Beetle. Their offer was $250. They called Pillsbury Baptist Bible College to confirm my employment and steady income. The school's financial officer assured the dealer about my reliability and employment contract.

The new VW Beetle was $1,300. My monthly installment was only fifty dollars, which I never had a problem paying. When I drove out of the dealership at noon, inhaling the new-car aroma, I praised the Lord for His goodness.

My job at Camp Chetek in Chetek, Wisconsin, was to serve as a counselor and drive the old camp truck to haul suitcases. I would follow the buses with the truck as they picked up campers. Each time the buses stopped, I loaded the campers' suitcases into the truck since there wasn't enough room for both them and their luggage on the bus.

I earned the nickname 'Sarge' by running my cabin like a military organization. Campers started as recruits and were promoted daily if they cooperated and stayed out of trouble.

When I went back to Milwaukee, I stayed at different churches and spoke to their teen groups. One weekend, I was at Faith Baptist Church in Waukesha. The pastor was Glen Teasdale. I happened to be there for the church's annual picnic. I filled my plate, then spotted a young lady sitting alone at a table. I decided to join her. This was the best decision I made since becoming a Christian.

I sat across from the beautiful teenage girl, Penny Stimpson, and we began to talk. She learned I had attended Western Baptist Bible College (WBBC), where I had made friends with people she knew. Penny had moved from California to Wisconsin six months before I started at WBBC.

Meeting Penny left a strong impression on me. She was lovely, dedicated to Jesus, and wanted to be a missionary—an exciting discovery for me. She was planning to attend Grand Rapids School of Bible and Music in Michigan, while I would be returning to Pillsbury. As she walked away, I felt my heart break. However, when I next saw her as a camp counselor, I was overjoyed. We performed different skits—mine about Japan, hers about Brazil—and I was once again impressed.

To my delight, instead of going to Grand Rapids, Penny chose to study at PBBC. Back at Pillsbury, I started dating one of Penny's best friends. After a few dates, she told me, "Tom, there's no future in our relationship. You're determined to be a missionary, and I'm not willing to leave the United States. My Russian parents sacrificed a lot to get here, and I won't dishonor them by leaving." This left me disappointed again.

Penny's friend told her about our breakup. Penny would

eventually tell me she hoped I would ask her out. She realized we shared the same goals and wanted to pursue them together.

*Penny always looked good, especially in black and pink. She knew this was my favorite color combination. I was always proud to be seen with her.*

In time, I did ask Penny out. After our first date, we both instantly knew we had found our lifelong partner. I told my roommates, "I'm going to marry this wonderful girl."

Penny was my most vocal wrestling fan. She loved the sport and would root me on from the stands. During Christmas vacation, we went to San Francisco. She stayed with a couple I knew, and I stayed with George. I worked delivering TVs, and we spent evenings together.

This next story is sad but worth sharing. For Christmas, I gave Penny a dictionary I had purchased from one of the students who spent the summer selling them. Her instant reaction showed disappointment. Realizing my mistake, I bought her perfume the next day. Penny later told me she had expected an engagement ring.

To get engaged during the school year, PBBC required the man to obtain written permission from the lady's father and then permission from Dr. Cedarholm, the school's president. I had not done either.

When we returned to school, I wrote to Bill Stimpson to ask permission to marry his daughter. After receiving his letter, I took it to Dr. Cedarholm for approval. Then, I arranged for one of Penny's friends to ask her to meet me in the chapel before the Wednesday night prayer meeting.

Upon arriving, Penny said, "I hope this is important, because I missed dinner."

"Sit down, please," I replied. Then, I asked, "Are you willing to go anywhere in the world to serve God as a missionary?"

"Yes."

I opened a ring box. "Will you marry me?"

She looked shocked. "Did you get permission from my dad and Dr. Cedarholm?"

"I certainly did," I assured her.

She accepted my proposal.

This is how the Latham missionary family began—a family deeply in love with Jesus, willing to serve Him anywhere in the world.

During Easter break, we traveled to Atlanta, Georgia, so I could meet Penny's family. Because I served in the military, her father, Bill Stimpson, immediately liked me. During our visit, we led Penny's sister, Karen, and her brother, Wayne, to Christ.

After the spring semester ended, we went to Waukesha, Wisconsin, to prepare for our wedding, scheduled for June 8. We had no money—Penny made her dress, and I borrowed a suit. Faith Baptist Church of Waukesha provided the food and cake. As I stood outside before the wedding, a flower truck arrived, the driver looking desperate.

"I can't find the address," he said. "These flowers are going to wilt in this extreme heat. Can I give them to this wedding?"

Without hesitation, I graciously accepted the flowers.

I offered Pastor Teasdale $25 to perform the ceremony. He gave it back to me, saying, "I think you need this more than I do." Our only cost was a five-dollar corsage I gave Penny.

Bill Stimpson had picked Penny up and then went to the mall to buy a tie. Because of this, she was half an hour late getting to the church. I was concerned she had changed her mind. (What a dreadful thought that was.) I felt fortunate to be marrying Penny. I couldn't bear the thought of it not happening.

*Penny and I started dating in October 1967. During our first date, we each decided the search for a life-time partner was over. This picture, from our wedding day, proves we were correct.*

A friend offered us a 'fishing lodge' in northern Minnesota for our honeymoon. We caught and ate fish. Six years later, Penny revealed she hated fish and had expected our accommodations to be nice. I was just as disappointed when the 'lodge' turned out to be a shanty.

The first conflict we had was over a can of sardines I had purchased. She sneered at me, "You aren't going to eat those here in the house, are you?"

"I was raised on Pepsi and sardines!" I countered. "Why can't I eat them in here?"

"You know my old roommate, Lois Dolittle, is coming soon," Penny replied. "Those nasty sardines will make the room, and maybe the whole house, stink like fish."

I thought I also had my rights, so I ate the sardines. She went into the bedroom, slammed the door, threw herself on the bed, and wept bitterly. I felt small enough to do jumping jacks under a dime! Later, I made it up to her.

We spent the summer working and continuing our ministry in Spring Valley. Penny had to quit working when she became pregnant with Thomas. When wrestling practice was moved to 3:00 PM, I quit because it interfered with my work schedule.

One Sunday morning, I asked Penny to fry the bacon. After a bit, she backed away from the skillet, "It's making popping sounds. I'm afraid of it," she said.

"Be brave, it's not going to splash on you."

She got closer. Just then, a bit of hot grease popped out, landing on the end of her nose.

"I told you!" she sobbed. "Now, I'm not going to church with you when I have this blister on the end of my nose." For the next 55 years, I fried the bacon myself, with Penny on the other side of the room.

Upon my graduation, we moved to Plymouth, Minnesota, where we started our youth pastor ministry at Plymouth Baptist Church. I began studying at Central Baptist Theological Seminary. We stayed in a house the church provided, and I was the church janitor.

On September 11, 1969, Thomas William Latham joined our family. We were delighted. The situation at the church, however, was not good. We decided to leave in June of 1970. I got a job at Northwestern Bell as a janitor, and we moved into a two-story house at 40th and Colfax, in Minneapolis.

By then, Penny was already pregnant with Shane, who was born on December 2, 1970. With two boys now, and Penny unable to have more children, we applied to adopt a newborn girl through Lutheran Social Services.

We began attending Highland Park Baptist Church located in St. Paul, Minnesota, where John Ballentine was pastor. He and his wife were marvelous people. We had a wonderful three years working with them.

In March of 1972, my mom wrote to me about my sister Harriet. She had been working for the San Francisco Mafia and wanted out. She sent Mom a letter asking for $50 for bus fare. She wrote, "The Mafia is running cocaine here, and I'm not interested in drugs. I'll come home and straighten out my life." The Mafia found out about it and threw her out of a fifteen-story window. Mom went to bury Harriet and got her $50 back from Western Union.

By the time I graduated from Central Seminary in May of 1973, we were already accepted as missionary candidates by Association of Baptists for World Evangelism (ABWE). After graduation, we sold all our furniture and went to candidate school at Clark Summit, Pennsylvania.

After four weeks of testing, we were approved as missionaries to Brazil. Now, all we had to do was raise $1,700 per month in support, as well as $5,000 for the initial outfit and passage.

*Penny is sitting by the fish we caught during our honeymoon in northern Minnesota. It was six years later when Penny eventually confessed to me that she didn't like anything about our fishing-trip honeymoon.*

# CHAPTER 12

# Deputation

While raising funds to go to Brazil, I worked at Grinnell Couplings in Minneapolis. To have a dependable vehicle for our deputation travel, we traded our Dodge van for a 1973 Ford Galaxy 500 station wagon. Back then, before seatbelts were mandatory, the boys could wander around inside the car as we traveled.

Initially, we stayed with the Sherie Ellsworth family. Later, a church member went to Florida and let us stay at their home.

Tina Swanson, a friend and a PBBC graduate, watched the boys while Pastor John Ballentine renewed our wedding vows at the house. Afterward, Penny and I went to a Ponderosa Steak House and then checked into a local motel. The next day, we attended the Big Ten Gymnastics Tournament at the University of Minnesota. She accepted this as a second honeymoon, making up for the first fiasco I perpetrated upon her at the 'fishing lodge.'

Veteran missionaries gave us a list of things to take to Brazil. We began accumulating necessities. I started scheduling meetings across the Midwest that would not interfere with my job. One meeting was in Brainerd, Minnesota, on a Wednesday night.

To get there in time, I left work an hour early. Penny picked me up, drove, and I changed clothes in the back seat during the two-hour drive. After our presentation, we drove back to Minneapolis, arriving at midnight, and I went to work the next day.

At another church in Minnesota, we learned their support for missionaries would be $500 a month—a surprising amount, almost one-third of the support we needed. After our visit, the deacons asked to meet with us. This was the only time a deacon board wanted to meet after our presentation, so we were excited.

During the meeting, a deacon remarked, "Brother Latham, your equipment list is so long it looks like you're taking everything with you."

"Several veteran missionaries recommended items on the list," I replied. (I'm thinking the $500 may now be $400 a month.)

Another deacon said, "I see you want a Sony reel-to-reel tape recorder. Why must it be Sony? Couldn't it be another brand?" (In my mind, our support estimate dropped further.)

"Sony is an international brand," I explained. "If the unit breaks down, I can get it fixed in Brazil."

He continued, "We think you should take any tape recorder, even if it doesn't work." (Probably $300 a month now)

I responded, "You want me to take a broken tape recorder to Brazil? The only broken thing I'll take is a broken heart for the Brazilian people."

Another deacon remarked, "Brother Latham, we believe Penny is called to be a missionary, but we're not sure about you." We didn't know this was part of the deacon's role.

I considered asking whether Penny could receive $250 a month and if it would be OK for me to accompany her. We left the meeting feeling wounded.

After 50 years of church-planting evangelism in Brazil, with four churches established—three with national pastors—we proved they misjudged us. Ironically, forty years later, that same church supported our son Shane and his wife, Erin.

That spring, we decided to live on the road and make our first trip to the West Coast. Calvary Baptist Church of San Francisco and several other Bay Area churches began to support us.

We presented our church-planting ministry at Lacomb Baptist Church in my hometown of Lacomb, Oregon. My mom attended. Nineteen years later, in the 1990s, the church treasurer—a neighbor since my birth—wrote, "Brother Tom, we've finally decided to support you. We just wanted to be sure you'd stick with it!"

After returning to Minneapolis, we bought a nineteen-foot trailer and traveled everywhere, including the East Coast. We lived in it until the freezing winter forced us inside our church nursery. A church in Michigan invited us to stay in their parsonage.

Before leaving for Clare, Michigan, we attended a mission conference in Lamberton, Minnesota. A blizzard trapped us, forcing us to abandon our car downtown and walk to the pastor's house, where we stayed for three days. Fourteen people died in that blizzard. We had no cell phones then.

When we dug out the car and opened the hood, the motor area was filled with snow. We had the points and plugs changed before heading to Clare. There, we stayed in a four-bedroom house, and I preached in many Regular Baptist churches in Michigan, Ohio, and Indiana.

Our candidate classmates thought Penny and I would be the first to reach the field, since I was seen as a type 'A' personality and both of us were go-getters. Yet, after two years of deputation, we had only forty percent of our support, while some classmates were already on their chosen field of ministry.

It had been five years since we applied to adopt a girl. We were frustrated. We thought our Lutheran Social Services caseworker disliked us, always keeping us at the bottom of the adoption list. A new case worker took over and called, "I can't believe you've been passed over for five years. You should have gotten a baby girl years ago. I'll fix this. In a month, you'll have your little princess."

We were scheduled for a mission conference in Elkhart, Indiana, but needed to fly to Minneapolis the same day to pick up our new baby girl, Kosette. A church member in Elkhart had a private plane and flew us all to Minnesota.

The caseworker handed us Kosette and explained we had to move to Minnesota and live there for a year before receiving her birth certificate. Now we understood why support-raising was taking so long—God wanted this special person in our family!

Another rule was that after one year, we would need to decide whether to keep Kosette. This seemed foolish—after a year with a baby, who would want to give her back?

After the Elkhart conference, we took 'Kosy' back to Clare, Michigan, and began preparing to move to Minneapolis.

BACK: PENNY AND TOM
FRONT: THOMAS JR. AND SHANE

*A Brazilian seamstress made these look-alike outfits for our deputation ministry. Notice how big Shane's bow tie is.*

*Oh no! Not a physical exam. Do we have to get shots?*

*Thomas did NOT like getting a shot to enter Brazil.*

# CHAPTER 13

## Physical Exams

The Brazilian government required us all to take physical exams from their designated doctor in Chicago. While still living in Clare, Michigan, I made appointments for our family of five. The cost was over $1,000.

The drive from Clare to Chicago was a 14-hour round trip. We left before dawn and arrived at the doctor's office with time to spare. While I was filling out paperwork, the nurse asked about our departure date for Brazil.

"In about a year from now."

"You can't take the exam."

"Why?"

"Because it's only valid for ninety days."

"What? No one told me this."

"No one told you the exam is only good for ninety days?"

"No! I'm working with the ABWE home office, the Northeast Brazil Field Council, and this office. None of you told me the exam would be good for only ninety days."

"Well, as you can see, you can't take the exam. It would be a waste of money."

"I can see that. So, what can I do?"

Following her advice, I called the Brazilian Consulate and explained my predicament. The woman on the phone suggested we still take the exams to avoid making another trip later. She advised asking the doctor not to date the forms until we were within ninety days of our departure, and to fill in the date at that time. (This was unlawful.)

Puzzled, I wondered: If it was so essential for us to get a physical exam, why would the consulate even suggest we engage in this illegal maneuver that would invalidate the exam results? It seemed they were not concerned about our health. Why did they make us travel fourteen hours to get the exam from their doctor? This was the first of many times I would question Brazilian government regulations and procedures!

We told the doctor we were sorry, but the exams would have to be canceled. Ten months later, we were back in the same office, taking the same exams. We were leaving for Brazil in thirty days. I learned a phrase while living in Minnesota that about covers this situation: *Whatever*!

Before getting a visa from the Brazilian Consulate, we all had to have a good-conduct statement from the police. Penny was concerned, saying, "I married a criminal! We're not going to Brazil." Reading further, the visa instructions said the report only needed to be from the police department in the city of our birth.

I went to jail in Ukiah, California; Medford, Oregon; and Hood

River, Oregon. Even though I did a lot of things that could have gotten me arrested in Lebanon, the city of my birth, I was never caught. It's evident to me now that God had His protective umbrella over me long before I was even interested in knowing Him.

We got our reports: Penny's was from the Detroit Police Department, and mine was from Lebanon, Oregon. We had to go to the Owatonna police for Thomas, the Minneapolis police for Shane, and the Spring Valley police for Kosy, since she was born there.

All three of the police departments in Minnesota laughed at us and told us to quit wasting their time. I appealed to each one in the same way: "If you don't give us a statement that our child has no police record, the Brazilian government won't give us a visa. Please, help us." They thought it was a stupid law, but still gave us the reports.

*Thomas (R) and Shane (striped shirt) with their friends before leaving for Brazil.*

## BRAZIL, SOUTH AMERICA

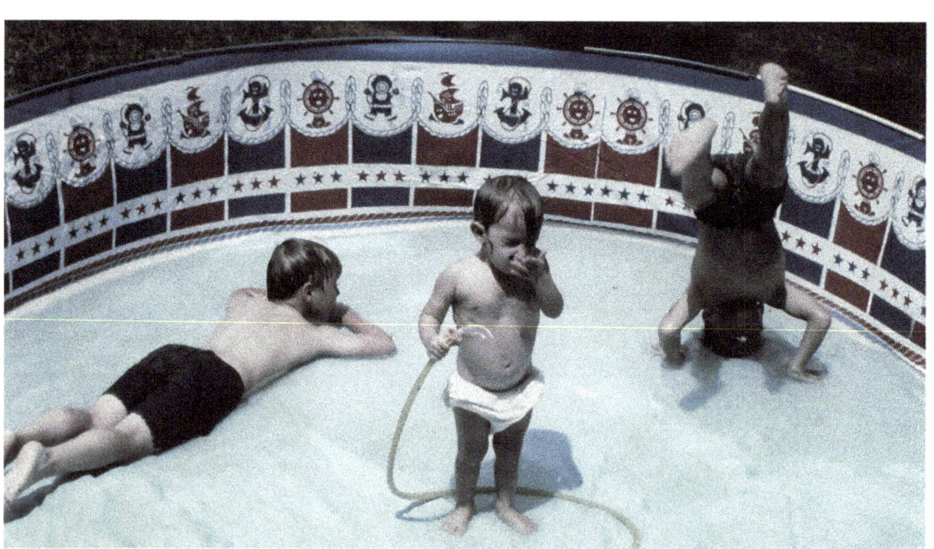

*Leaving Minnesota in October and arriving during the Brazilian summer required getting a swimming pool and trying to stay cool. This was in Fortaleza while I was in language school.*

# CHAPTER 14

## Arriving in Brazil

After buying a Collins KWM-2 ham radio and a 1000-watt power booster, I focused on getting my FCC Amateur Radio Service License. I studied every book I could find and traveled from Clare, Michigan, to Lansing to take a fifty-question test. I was allowed to miss six questions, but I had never studied six of the fifty questions.

"Lord, you know how hard I've studied," I prayed. "I need to get five of these six questions right, or I'll fail. Help me." I went 'Eeny Meeny Miny Moe' on the multiple-choice test. I must have gotten five right because I passed. Thank You, Lord, for helping me.

The license required copying Morse code at 13 words per minute, which I practiced for 2 years. Although I could do it, nerves caused me to fail four times. With one week left before our flight to Brazil, I had one last chance. Again, I asked for help from above.

As I sat there anxiously waiting, the monitor said, "We're going to give the twenty-one-word test first. Those taking the thirteen-word test can also participate." This was the help I needed. I copied twenty-one words a minute. When I took my test, I wasn't nervous, and I passed. Thank You, Lord, for helping me.

Highland Park Baptist Church in Saint Paul, Minnesota had

moved to Bryant Avenue in south Minneapolis. We started stockpiling our baggage at the unsold church building in St. Paul.

I packed our belongings into fourteen crates and twenty steel barrels. Afterwards, I found out the Brazilian Consulate required a detailed list of each item in every crate and barrel, so I repacked everything. Then, needing the serial numbers for every item that had one, I had to unpack, then repack a third time.

Bryant Avenue Baptist Church was selling the building, so I moved our crates and barrels to Mrs. Lillian Payne's garage in Owatonna, Minnesota.

We had a whole year to raise the rest of our support. We made a trip to the West Coast so my grandparents and mother could meet Kosy, our new daughter. After the required waiting period was up, we met with the judge and assured him we wanted to keep Kosy. The boys even voted "yes!"

Ready to leave for Brazil, we rented a Ryder truck and loaded our baggage with help from college students. A student commented, "I think the truck is over the weight limit. If it is, the weigh station will force you to leave items behind."

At the feed-weighing center, it turned out our baggage was overweight, as the student predicted. We removed 13 barrels, loaded 8 into a U-Haul trailer, and shipped the other 5 barrels separately to a New Orleans freight company.

In early October, our family climbed into the Ryder truck and drove to New Orleans. We were exhausted but excited to finally be on our way. As it turned out, the student was right about the weigh stations along the route; we were stopped five times.

Arriving in New Orleans, I needed two parking spots for the truck and trailer, close to the Norwegian Freight Company in downtown New Orleans. Two attendants told me to move, saying, "Get that thing out of here."

I prayed to find suitable parking. Against all odds, I found the needed spaces. Penny and the kids waited while I paid $4,000 to ship our baggage.

At the docks, I detached the trailer so dockworkers could unload the truck, and then they unloaded the trailer. While reconnecting the trailer, I was called to the freight office about the five barrels we were shipping.

After leaving, the trailer came loose—I'd forgotten to connect the ball correctly when I returned from the freight office. The trailer swung back and forth but stayed attached by the chain (fortunately, I had connected the safety chain correctly). We were lucky it didn't cause an accident, and we thanked the Lord for keeping us safe.

We spent the last week with Penny's parents in Atlanta, Georgia. After we got to the airport, ready to fly to Brazil, we discovered we had left our medical X-rays at the home of Penny's parents. Bill Stimpson rushed back across Atlanta, got the X-rays, and handed them to me as I was getting on the plane. In Rio de Janeiro, the authorities asked for those X-rays. Thank You, God!

Upon arrival in Miami, Varig officials said we lacked confirmed seats because of a requirement I didn't know about. We appealed and secured five seats.

We landed in Belem, Brazil. Rick McClain, a pilot with Baptist Mid-Missions, helped us through customs. We had my ham radio padded with Kosy's Pampers. The customs officials thought that was funny. The temperature was intolerable, and the humidity almost unbearable.

During our trip from the airport to our destination, I reflected on the Herculean effort it had taken to reach Brazil. I prayed we would make a meaningful difference and bring glory to God. After what felt like a mini-eternity, we approached Fortaleza, Brazil, where we were scheduled to spend a year learning Portuguese.

We arrived on a Monday. Exhausted, Penny and the kids fell asleep at the guest house. Without a vehicle, we couldn't get to the house we were renting 10 miles away.

That night, the Minnesota Vikings were playing the Los Angeles Rams. I borrowed a short-wave radio to listen to the game on Armed Forces Network. Staying up until midnight, I heard when the Vikings won 11-10. The next day, we ran around handling paperwork. The heat was awful.

I had brought $10,000 in cash for another missionary. It was sewn into my pants pocket. This amount was allowed by the government. I asked the missionary if I could borrow $3,000 to purchase a 1976 VW bus with only 3,000 kilometers on it. The missionary loaned us the money.

Mike Burnside, a friend in Meadville, Pennsylvania, had saved enough money to buy himself a new car. When he heard that we didn't have the funds for the vehicle we needed and had borrowed money from another missionary, he gave us his money. Thank You, Lord, for providing us with the funds for a vehicle. Mike's gift helped two ministries, because it allowed me to pay the missionary back sooner than we had initially planned.

We moved into a large house on a Christian campground that had once belonged to a state governor. Our baggage was delayed for seven months, leaving us short on clothes.

We had already been renting the house for three months. I had nine months to finish language school, or we would have to sign another contract for a full year. I started language school the next day.

Penny and I attended classes in the morning, while the boys attended Baptist Mid-Missions' School for Missionary Kids (MKs). We had a Brazilian lady taking care of Kosy, whose first language would be Portuguese, when she began to talk.

Back when we were in candidate school, Penny and I took a language aptitude test. In four hours, we had to pick up enough vocabulary and grammar to answer a few questions. The test used a non-existent language. On a scale of zero to one hundred, Penny got ninety-five; my score was zero. (They didn't want to give me less than zero, because they didn't want to hurt my feelings.)

ABWE told us we could only go to a Spanish-speaking or Portuguese-speaking country. Nothing changed; we were already headed to Brazil. God knew all about my lack of language-learning ability. I told our friends at ABWE not to underestimate me. Even though I didn't have the God-given gift of languages, I could learn any language, given enough time. I have a quality that others may not have—it's called tenacity, or perseverance— good old fashioned 'stick-to-it-iveness.'

Saturdays were our family days. We went to the beach, downtown, or shopping. Everything was new to us.

Our baggage came seven months later. We asked the other missionaries at the language school to help us bring our luggage to the campgrounds. They told us they didn't have time to help us and suggested we ask the Brazilians for help. We asked the church's people. They were glad to help us. To show our gratitude, we bought them barbecued chicken.

*Our baggage finally joined us in Brazil.*
*Shane, Kosy, and Thomas were the inspection team.*

*The kids were trying to cool off in the blazing heat.*

# CHAPTER 15

# Our First Ministry

We faced many tropical health issues. Shane discovered parasites crawling in and out of the skin on his elbow. Kosy vomited a tapeworm. Thomas developed a worm under his skin. We all ended up with head lice; therefore, we became regular customers at the local pharmacy.

The house posed its own challenges. It was infested with tarantulas, cockroaches, and giant rats that chewed through screens to enter at night. Since we were not warned about these issues, adjusting was difficult, especially for Penny, though she managed to cope.

Five huge German Shepherds guarded the campground. They were friendly enough to us, but ran loose all night to keep unwanted personnel out. We bought a dog that was half German Shepherd and named him Samson.

Monkeys would jump from one palm tree to another. I threw a coconut at one, knocking him to the ground. We put that monkey in a cage, but he didn't like being behind bars! He finally chewed his way out of the cage, but didn't make it to the tree before Samson ended his young life.

Beth Peace, a nurse, visited the Amazon and brought back two parrots. She boarded the plane with one parrot under each arm. We put one of the parrots in the cage. The bird also didn't like it. Its escape was followed by a short chase by Samson, ending up badly for the fowl.

I've always had a passion for Minnesota Twins baseball and Minnesota Vikings football. I also followed the University of Minnesota Gophers in football and wrestling. Hanging by the desk in my study was a large photo of Fran Tarkenton. In the picture, it was snowing as he was throwing the football.

On Sundays, I could pick up Armed Forces Network and hear a football game. I was listening once when the announcer said, "Something's wrong. The San Francisco 49ers are beating the Vikings 20-0 during a snowstorm in Minneapolis." The announcer repeated, "This doesn't seem right to me." Listening to the announcer, I was shocked.

Later, the announcer said, "Something strange happened in Minneapolis. Bud Grant pulled Tarkenton out, close to the end of the third quarter, and put rookie Tommy Kramer on the field. Now with three minutes to go, the Vikings are leading 21-20." Tommy always had a great end-game mentality.

In the fall of 1976, after one month in Portuguese language school, Penny dropped out. Since she already spoke Spanish, she picked up Portuguese quickly. I went to school for the next eight months, also studying on weekends and holidays. I finished language school in June of 1977. I knew being proficient in Portuguese would take me a few more years of serious study.

After hiring two trucks, we moved our belongings to Mossoró, which lies halfway between Fortaleza and Natal, the capital of Rio Grande do Norte. We rented a house across from a public school. Ironically, the house had several fruit trees but no kitchen sink. The owner assured us he would provide one.

I made a mosquito net to fit over the kids' bunk beds. Penny and I slept under a net as well. We had only one window air conditioner, installed in our bedroom.

Mossoró's location, just five hundred miles from the equator, meant extreme heat year-round. Even the well water reached 155° Fahrenheit. We lived there for three years, and during the last two, it did not rain at all.

We were required by the Association of Baptists for World Evangelism (ABWE) to work for one year under a veteran missionary. This assignment led us to partner with someone who had attended Western Baptist Bible College with me, which in turn led us to choose Mossoró.

After six months working with our assigned veteran missionary, we realized it was not a good fit. We discovered an old church building that had been closed. This was ABWE's oldest established church in the area. Over twenty-seven years, it had seen twenty-seven missionaries and pastors, and was now empty.

We contacted the five ladies who were still members of the church. They decided to call Penny and me to reopen the work. These ladies were very patient with my struggling Portuguese.

One of the first problems we encountered was bats flying around the auditorium while I was preaching. Occasionally, a bat would hit the overhead fan, which caused a lot of disturbance. We had to get rid of the bats.

Taking off all the ceramic roofing tile, the boys and I used tennis rackets and barrel lids to kill one hundred eighty bats. This gave us a better 'batting average' than the Chicago Cubs!

The church needed a serious clean-up job and a lot of paint. One night, we were painting benches when Eurides came in with her brother. "I was saved in this church many years ago. I went to the United States with my American bosses. Now, I'm a janitor at Moody Bible Institute. I came to visit my family and heard the church was open again. This is my brother Zizi."

They helped us paint. The next day, as was my custom with new people, I visited Zizi in his home. He was swinging in a hammock, smoking a cigarette. I had already learned that one could be blunt with Brazilians. "Your sister said you are a Christian. I'm wondering when you're going to get your heart right with God."

He pointed to the kitchen, where his wife was working, and said, "When that thing in the kitchen gets saved, I'll get my heart right with God."

Then I heard a voice from the kitchen: "When that man who is swinging in the hammock and smoking gets his heart right with God, I'll get saved." That was Branquinha, his wife.

Seeing their stalemate, I addressed Zizi directly: "Zizi, the burden is on your shoulders. If you're a Christian, you need to get your heart right with God. When you do, I believe she will become a follower of Christ."

Zizi threw his cigarette in the corner and promised, "I'll get my heart right with God."

They started coming to church. One Sunday night, Penny asked Branquinha if she wanted to be saved. She said, "Tomorrow, I'll go to your house and be saved." Neither Penny nor I had ever heard anyone say this. Penny tried to get a decision out of her that night, but she was firm about doing it the next day.

Early the next morning, Zizi rode his bicycle to our house. On the back of his bike, his wife had a python-like grip around his waist to keep herself from falling off. She had a big grin on her face when she hopped off the bike and said, "Let's go see Susana (Penny's Brazilian name). That bumpy ride was worth it to keep my promise to her." She prayed with Penny and gave her heart to Jesus. Both Zizi and Branquinha came to all the services, bringing their four children.

> **Consider how precious a soul must be when both God and the devil are after it.**

*I worked in the blazing sun during our first term in Northeast Brazil.*

*Zizi painting the benches in our first church the first time I met him.*

*DOCA (SOBER)*

> *"Therefore if any man be in Christ, he is a new creature: old things are passed away; behold, all things are become new."*
>
> *2 Corinthians 5:17*

# CHAPTER 16

## Doca the Drunk

One Sunday afternoon, I visited Zizi's family. As I was leaving, my Honda motorcycle had a flat tire, so I left it and started walking home. Halfway there, I saw a man staggering toward me. He bumped into me, draped his arm around my shoulder, and his breath, heavy with alcohol, shocked me.

"What are you doing?" I asked him.

"I'm Zizi's friend," he mumbled.

I value friendship evangelism, so I decided to help him get back to Zizi's house.

Zizi explained, "This is Doca, my friend. He owns the little store across the street and drinks a lot of alcohol."

Branquinha made coffee.

I joked, "Let's see how many cups of coffee he can drink before church tonight." I left Doca with Zizi and went home to prepare for the evening service.

That night, Doca attended church and went forward during the invitation. I took him to my office, where he accepted Christ as Savior. When he returned home, he poured out all of his liquor. The change in him was immediate and lasting.

I visited him every other day, checking to see if he remained sober. His lifestyle transformation was remarkable. Word spread: "Doca the drunk had found religion."

About two weeks later, three ladies came to church. After the service, they walked up to the pulpit. One of them asked, "What's going on here? First, Zizi stops smoking, and Branquinha becomes a Christian. Then, that drunk Doca gets saved and pours his liquor down the drain. Again, I ask, what's going on here?"

I was happy to answer them. "We preach the gospel here. The gospel teaches that everyone is a sinner. To go to heaven, our sins need forgiveness. There is only one way: accepting what Jesus did for us on the cross. That's called 'being born again'. This leads to a real change in a person's heart and life. That's what happened with Doca."

The women were Grace, Linda, and Lordes. Penny listened as they prayed for salvation. In just three weeks, evangelism was spreading rapidly. The women invited me to preach in front of Grace's house. We set up a platform with plywood and barrels, connected a one-hundred-watt bulb, and used my small sound system.

Since we were so close to the equator, the sun set at 5:30 PM and rose at 5:30 AM every day of the year. So, at 6:00 PM, it was already dark.

Life in Northeast Brazil is very different from other regions of the country, much like the difference between Minnesota and Alabama. As I began preaching, a crowd gathered. Some may have simply wanted to hear the 'Gringo's' American accent.

This style of evangelism was new for the Latham family. Later that month, Grace's husband, Divaldmir, became a Christian, and soon after, Linda's husband did as well.

A month later, while visiting someone in jail, I saw Grace sitting on a bench by the entrance, crying. I asked what had happened, but she only cried harder. Inside, I saw her husband, Divaldmir, in a cell. Shocked, I asked him, "What are you doing here?"

He replied, "I can tell you, but I don't think you'll believe me."

"Tell me your story," I said.

Without hesitation, he told me his tale, and he was right; I did have a hard time believing him. I thought, however, that giving him the benefit of the doubt was the best move. "I believe your account," I assured him.

"Good—now go outside and talk my wife into believing my story."

Returning to her side, I said, "Grace, I heard his version."

She was still sobbing, "He's no good. My parents warned me. I don't believe him."

I encouraged her, "Grace, if he's lying, we'll find out soon. But right now, he needs your support. Penny and I will be here with you. If you trust him for now, we can move forward and find a solution." She took my advice. Mutual trust returned and their marriage was secured.

*The first church we started was in the northeastern corner of Brazil, in the blazing-hot city of Mossoró. Well water was 155 degrees. Year-round weather was unbearably hot.*

*Before I baptized Grace, we had to let the water cool off. Near the equator, we were sitting over a thin layer of earth above a source of tremendous molten heat.*

# CHAPTER 17

## Strange Customs

### Death and Burial Customs

Divaldmir and Grace had a baby who died eighteen days after being born. In Northeast Brazil, mothers do not attend their babies' burials. Children typically place the body in a shoebox with strings to carry it to the cemetery. We witnessed this several times.

Since Grace was absent and Divaldmir could not leave work, Penny and I took the baby's shoebox to the cemetery. The caretaker began digging the grave; during this, we were shocked to find a human skull in the dirt.

After the burial, Divaldmir arrived and asked me to speak. I referenced *2 Samuel 12:23* and noted biblical assurances of babies' safety in God's care. Later, Grace named her next daughter Susana, after Penny's Brazilian name, Susana.

As we left, a teenager challenged my teaching about the soul's destiny after death, offering to visit and discuss biblical interpretations.

I put my hand on his shoulder. "Son, I've had four years of Greek and two years of Hebrew language training, while studying the Bible formally for twelve years. I'll continue to believe what I know to be the truth."

A few months later, a Brazilian pastor across town called me. "Pastor Thomas," he said, "an older man in our church passed away. We have only a paper coffin for burial. If we push it to the church in this rain, there will be nothing left of the coffin. Can you bring your VW bus to help us get the coffin to the church?"

*MOVING A PAPER COFFIN*

"Yes, I can do that."

"Can you also bring your 35 mm camera?"

Upon arrival at the church, they removed the coffin's lid and propped up the grandfather's head so the grandchildren could take a final photo with him. Each grandchild put an arm around his neck for a touching picture. The reason for needing my camera became clear.

After I took all their pictures, one of the grandchildren asked me if I wanted my photo taken with Grandpa. I declined, telling them I hardly knew him. The family resettled the grandfather into the coffin and replaced the lid.

Penny was visiting people in the neighborhood one day and saw a woman sitting in her doorway, crying. Approaching her, Penny asked, "May I come in and pray with you?"

The woman was mourning her father's death. To make space for Penny to sit and pray with her, she shifted her father's body on the couch. Penny remained unfazed and offered her support.

In Brazil, there is no embalming, and the family must handle all burial arrangements, ensuring the body is buried within a day. The wake lasts overnight so relatives can pay their respects.

Immediate family members often stay up all night during the wake, leaving them exhausted by the time of the burial. This exhaustion can cause some to faint.

After another church couple lost a baby, the wife fainted, and the husband focused on her care. Penny and I managed the burial arrangements, a task beyond our ministry training.

**Introduction and Greeting Customs**

In Southern Brazil, introductions are intimate, especially among acquaintances. The first kiss on a woman's left cheek means 'Hello.' The second, on the right, means 'How are you?' Teenage girls receive a third kiss on the left, which is a wish for marriage. Engaged women get another one on the right, hoping they avoid living with their mother-in-law—a common occurrence after marriage.

Across Brazil, strangers commonly exchange hearty handshakes. Among friends, greetings involve hugs and backslaps. I appreciate these customs; handshakes can be impersonal in some cultures, but a bear hug and backslap are genuine and meaningful.

*Doctors, who were my English students, attended a Christmas program in our first church.*

*Ready for a water skiing story?*

# CHAPTER 18

# Water Skiing in Brazil

Some experiences on the mission field surprised us. My English classes for medical doctors in Mossoró were going well, and we became friends with all of them. One Sunday afternoon, Dr Luiz Batista invited us to his property for a birthday celebration. When we arrived, we discovered his entire family was at the river running through his land.

As we approached the river, we saw a humorous scene: a motorboat was slowly pulling a man whose head was barely above the water. Dr Batista explained, "Thomas, I bought this boat and skis to use today, but no one can manage to get out of the water. I suppose all Americans know how to water ski, right?"

"Well, I do," I replied. "What can I do to help you?"

"If you really know how to ski, please take that man's place and show us how it's done. I've been here all morning, losing face with my whole family."

He was delighted that I was going to 'save his face,' as he so poetically stated it. I put on the safety jacket, grabbed the handle, sat on the dock, and told the boat driver to give it the whole thing. I told him to put the gas lever to the limit, all the way forward.

I should have known what was going on before when the driver asked, "Are you sure? The whole amount? All the way forward?"

"Yes, give it all you've got. Now."

He did precisely that, and I shot off the dock, managing to stand up as the crowd on the beach cheered. However, it's important to note: we were on a river, not a lake. As we continued upstream, the river became narrower.

I started to wonder how we would return to the crowd when I saw the driver turn the boat around and pass me, heading downstream. Because I liked my armpits where they were since birth, I let go and sank into the river. Thankfully, there was not a horde of bloodthirsty piranhas in the area.

When he came back, I explained, "You need to make a wide sweep so I can turn around. Do you understand?" He assured me he did.

I got back on the skis, and made a successful circle near the beach while the relatives clapped and cheered. We then went upstream again. This time, I went from water to sand, from sand to water, from water to sand, and back to water again. Throughout this little adventure, I managed to stay up with my armpits intact.

The doctor thanked me for saving his face. We went back to the house and had a lovely birthday dinner.

# CHAPTER 19

## White Hand

During a teen activity in Mossoró, João and Lucas arrived to play volleyball. João was a little tipsy, so I told him to sit out. He returned sober to the next activity. After a few services, he became somewhat of a regular.

Our family had to go to Natal for a field council meeting at the camp on Bom Fim Lake. We didn't arrange for a house sitter, but we did ask the public school guard to keep an eye on our place. He later called to say someone had tried to rob us, but he scared them off. Penny took the kids and returned home to find my ham radio and other items stacked in the living room.

Everyone at church knew we would be gone for three days, including João and Lucas. Suspecting them, I went to see João.

"You and Lucas tried to rob us, didn't you?" I asked.

"It wasn't me. It was Lucas," he insisted.

I then found Lucas. "João said you tried to rob our house."

"No, it wasn't me. João did it."

It wasn't hard to figure out that both were involved. They stopped coming to church after that. Brazil has a serious crime problem, especially house robberies. When minors are caught, judges often let them go with only a warning.

The Mossoró police got tired of this. They formed an off-duty vigilante group called *White Hand.* This group would find criminals, especially murderers, kill them, and leave a white handprint on their chest as a warning to others.

One day, João came running to our house. "Pastor, you must help me. The radio announcer read the names of people on the *White Hand* list. My name is on that list. I am doomed."

I felt sorry for João, even after he tried to rob us. I told him, "If you come to all our church services, I'll find *White Hand* and ask them to take you off the list. I mean it—I'll help you, but you have to be here so we can convince them you won't return to crime."

João agreed, but he never showed up. I still thought he deserved another chance, so I went to his house. No one answered when I knocked. Trying his neighbor, I asked, "Do you know where João is?"

The neighbor smirked and said, "Last I saw, he was climbing the backyard wall while men from *White Hand* knocked at the front door. I don't think we'll ever see him again." And we didn't.

Contributing to the seriousness of the crime problem in Brazil, judges rarely jail minors, even if they commit multiple serious crimes. Gangs use minors because of this. Nearly everyone in our church has been robbed. In 2023, our Brazilian president even said, "No one is going to jail for stealing a cell phone."

We always insisted that Christ coming into our lives will produce a new person. I often used my own life as an example of this dramatic change. When we were packing to leave Brazil for our first furlough, our boys helped me take some of our things to a charity drop. Two ladies from a liturgical church approached me. One asked, "You're Pastor Thomas from the Baptist Church, aren't you?"

"I am. How can I help you?"

The other lady continued the conversation: "We know what happened to that drunk Doca. We also noticed the others who were affected by his lifestyle change. We don't see those kinds of results in our church work. We'd like to see those kinds of results."

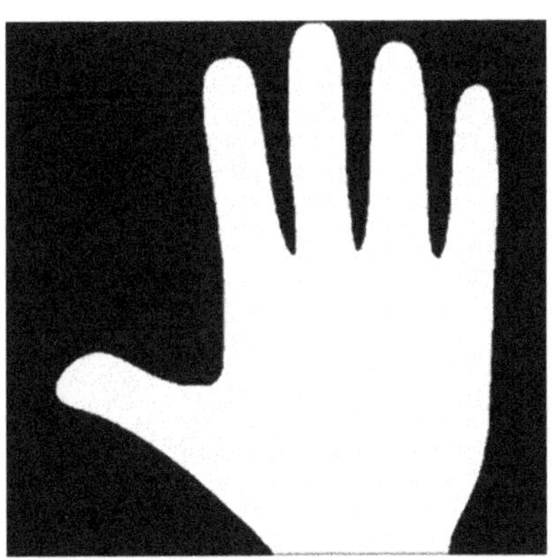

SYMBOL OF THE
"WHITE HAND" GROUP

*PEOPLE AT OUR FIRST CHURCH IN MOSSORÓ 1980*

*OUR FAMILY AT CAMP IN MOSSORÓ*

*"Search me, O God, and know my heart: try me, and know my thoughts: And see if there be any wicked way in me, and lead me in the way everlasting."*

*Psalm 139:23-24*

# CHAPTER 20

# From Chaos to Tranquility

## A Character Reboot

Although I was a seasoned Christian with years of Bible training, God needed me to address some persistent flaws—especially pride. Despite growing up humble and poor and spending time on Grandpa Taylor's farm in Oregon, I was not as humble as my experiences might suggest.

After language school, we moved to Mossoró, in Rio Grande do Norte, to begin missionary work. As newcomers, our mission organization, Association of Baptists for World Evangelism (ABWE), required us to spend our first year under the leadership of a veteran missionary. We quickly realized this arrangement was not what we signed up for.

We soon recognized that the veteran missionary we worked with struggled with organization and personnel management, often leaving tasks unfinished. His reputation revealed that a continued partnership was unsustainable.

We found a local church that had closed after 27 years. Over the years, 27 full-time workers had come and gone. When the last missionary couple left to start a new church, this church closed its doors.

We contacted four ladies who were still members; they all agreed to ask us to come and reopen the church. My Portuguese was awful, but the ladies had no lack of patience as I spoke and preached. We knew we were violating the rules set down by ABWE; we also knew it was impossible to continue working with the veteran missionary.

Progress was slow because I struggled with Portuguese, but we were moving forward and saw successes, as described earlier. I felt overwhelming joy knowing we could help establish a church that would soon support a Brazilian pastor—all within three years.

Success in reviving the church exposed my most significant flaw: pride. I even told Penny that we'd return to the States as heroes for starting a church in our first term—something many never accomplish. Penny didn't challenge my arrogance, and perhaps agreed. I never asked.

Pride nearly destroyed our marriage. We masked our struggles before others, but privately, we were at a breaking point and decided to return to the States for marriage counseling.

We reached out to Dr. Wendell Kempton, president of ABWE, and explained our situation. He told us to return to the States immediately and promised to help us find a marriage counselor.

Uncertain of our future, we sold what we could, stored the rest, and returned to the States—not as heroes, but feeling defeated.

After arriving in Atlanta, Georgia, we set up our new home with items purchased with the proceeds from selling our belongings in Brazil. Dr. Howard Eyrich became our marriage counselor. We enrolled the kids in a Christian day school and began attending counseling sessions.

Dr. Kempton was a real gentleman. He had advised us to take six months' leave. We were to have no furlough meetings and focus on getting our marriage back on track. We attended counseling sessions once a week and spent the rest of the time putting the rebuilding principles into practice.

I had a lot of free time. The counselor told me to get a job. I worked at a Burger King drive-through. This was not a place where customers could sit down. I made French fries. Penny even came to work for one day, but had to quit because she was facing some serious surgery.

While Penny recovered from surgery, we continued to practice the biblical principles Dr. Eyrich taught us. After six months, we felt our marriage was repaired. I wasn't yet a humble man, but I was working towards it.

We expected to be cleared for furlough. Dr. Kempton approved and advised me to share honestly with supporting pastors about our marriage struggles and recovery, assuring me they would understand.

Penny remained in Atlanta, and I started visiting our churches. The first pastor I met was Mike Whitesell, who wrote the introduction to this book. He was exceptionally kind and gave me great hope that we would be okay with our restoration process.

After visiting several churches, I headed back to Atlanta with great aspirations, thinking we would be all right. This was when our field director came to Atlanta to tell us we had been put on a two-year leave of absence to work out our problems. We thought he might want to talk to our marriage counselor, but he didn't. The marriage counselor asked him to join us for lunch, where he explained to our field director our journey from chaos to tranquility.

The field director was not impressed and told us we were on a leave of absence with no hope of a future with ABWE. I asked him why. He said, "You need time to spend with your family; we're going to give you that time."

I replied, "If I quit furlough and don't report to my churches, I'll have to get a full-time job. If I do this, I'd be working 40 hours a week. That would be 40 fewer hours with my family. I don't see how this fits into your idea of my spending more time with my family."

Dismissal from ABWE came swiftly. The organization mailed letters about our leave to all supporters, and only two of 25 churches continued their support.

We moved to Morrow, Georgia, where I got a job as an electrician with a Christian company. As I was working, I glanced at the wire strippers in my hand. I looked up to heaven and prayed, "God, please take this tool out of my hand and put a Bible back in it."

Our shared love for Jesus and desire to serve as missionaries never wavered, even as we stopped caring for each other. We chose to repair our relationship—and succeeded.

Needing a path back to Brazil, we applied to Baptist World Mission (BWM). The new Executive Director, Dr. Fred Moritz, was someone we knew personally from our days as youth directors at a church near his. We'd often worked together at church events.

We submitted our applications and were accepted as candidates, though we still felt unsure about God's direction. I requested that the mission board put a hold on our application. Dr. Moritz called to ask why.

"Doc, I'm not sure where we go from here."

"Come and work with us. I want to come to Atlanta to see you."

"That might be a waste of your time."

"Tom, let me decide if it is a waste of my time. I'm coming."

"Okay. Come and see us."

When Dr. Moritz pulled into our driveway and got out of the car, Penny and I noticed Dr. Monroe Parker, the Director Emeritus, was with him. This surprised us. We had a good talk with them and explained our journey from chaos to recovery. They were very kind and said they wanted us to follow through and present ourselves to Baptist World Mission.

We both felt we couldn't return to Brazil unless we moved back to Minnesota and worked out of our home church, Bryant Ave Baptist Church in South Minneapolis. We packed up and moved to Minnesota.

I got a job at an apple processing plant right across the street from where we lived. Penny got a job as the church secretary. We had lived in the Midwest before; we knew we were headed for below-zero temps and a lot of snow. September came, and the kids started school at Bryant Avenue Christian Academy. During this time, the boys had a paper route until it got TOO cold to do it.

At the board meeting in Michigan that October, Dr. B. Myron Cedarholm endorsed us, recalling personal memories from my wrestling days with the Pillsbury Comets. Pastor Dr. Clarke Poorman, one of the few who continued supporting us, seconded the motion. The board voted unanimously to accept us as missionaries.

Determined to return to Brazil, we spent two years traveling the USA raising support. By October 1983, we had what we needed and departed for Southern Brazil to start a new church in Restinga, Rio Grande do Sul, a city of 220,000 residents. It was cowboy country, the land of the Gauchos.

BRAZILIAN GAUCHO

TOM AND PENNY ON FURLOUGH

*Sherie Ellsworth housed us various times and Thomas for a full year of ACE school.*

RESTINGA CHURCH PEOPLE

*Shane going into the Restinga church.*

# CHAPTER 21

# Luzia and Dude

In October 1980, we left Mossoró for our first furlough. During that time, we switched mission boards and joined Baptist World Mission in Decatur, Alabama. During this furlough we lost 90% of our support, so we had to restart the deputation process. For the next two years, we traveled around the United States. In October 1983, we finally arrived in Rio Grande do Sul, Brazil's southernmost state.

We rented a missionary's house when we arrived, but he would return in four months. That meant we urgently needed to find a new place to live. Penny learned the government was offering a fifteen-year loan for new homeowners. I found a house being built just four blocks away. We secured the loan and became proud owners of a new home.

At that stage, I had been a Christian for twenty years and a missionary for nine. We had spent sixteen years following God's will. Despite all our efforts, our only earthly possession had been a car. Now we had a four-bedroom, three-bathroom house with a swimming pool, which delighted the kids.

Penny and I worked in Restinga, a city of 220,000 people that was only two miles wide. Our church building was small but well-located on the main thoroughfare.

## Luzia

Six months into the pastorate of our second church, Luzia walked through the door. "I'm looking for the true church," she said with a winning smile.

"This church teaches the Bible as we understand it," I replied. "Maybe you've found the right church for you."

I always get visitors' names and addresses so I can visit them before the following Sunday. I did that for Luzia, but then lost her address. I prayed, "Lord, excuse my lack of organization. Please bring her back so I can learn where she lives." She didn't return the next Sunday, which made me quite frustrated with myself.

The following Sunday, to my amazement, Luzia returned to church. Penny and I visited her home. I explained the plan of salvation and asked if she would like to pray. She agreed, and we bowed our heads. She prayed silently for a long time, which didn't bother me. I eventually asked if she was done. "No, I'm not finished yet," she replied.

When she was done, Luzia looked up, smiled, and said, "Now, I'm finished."

Very few times in my life have I seen such a quick and long-lasting conversion. Luzia worked on a computer at a hardware store. She also spent three hours a day on the bus, traveling back and forth to work. I was astonished to learn that during this time on the bus, she memorized whole chapters of the Bible.

I was visiting members in Restinga one day, where I let Shane ride my Honda dirt bike around town. A while later, I saw him running on the road. I thought this was not a good sign. "Hey, Shane, where's my bike?"

"I left the key in it, and Luzia's pothead brother stole it."

Luzia said she wasn't coming back to church because of the shame her brother brought upon her by stealing my bike. We talked her out of that bad idea.

Two weeks later, the police told me they found the bike. We went to see it. John, a policeman, told me if I bought them some beer and barbecue, I could have the bike immediately. If not, I would have to wait two weeks to get it. I refused his offer and went home without the bike.

Later, I realized my bike could disappear from the police pound, so I decided to call. "Is this John?" I asked. He confirmed. "I'll bring Coca-Cola and barbecue for the bike." He sounded wary and said he didn't know what I meant. Worried he was caught in a sting, he denied everything. Two weeks later, I got the bike back.

After that, Luzia stood up in church and said, "I was horribly embarrassed when my no-good, drugged-up brother stole the pastor's bike. He then stole someone else's bike, and was killed. He was an evil influence on our family. I'm glad his influence is gone."

Luzia started tithing and learned how to play the guitar. She was soon playing special music in the church. After about four months, while we were singing, "I Am Happy in the Service of the King," she was crying.

I asked her why she was crying. "Because I'm not in the service of the King. I want to be in the ministry full-time." I was in favor of this.

A young man named Ernesto Bezerra from Mossoró wrote to us, expressing a desire to work with our church. Penny and I bought a $2,000 house and turned it into a parsonage. Ernesto joined us as my assistant. After some time, we suggested he and Luzia consider marrying. They were married four months later.

## A young woman named Dude

Luzia began evangelizing her family. Some of her cousins came to Christ. João Luiz was one. He came to church with his wife and helped us with some youth projects.

Luzia became pregnant. She and Ernesto had a girl, and named her after Penny's middle name, Susana. Now, in Rio Grande do Sul, we have a second Brazilian baby named after Penny. This showed how much Brazilians loved Penny Sue Latham.

Luzia's mom and sister, Dude, got saved. Penny noticed Dude was not coming to our Sunday evening service. "Are you attending another church?"

"No, I'm going to dances to find a husband."

Penny didn't hesitate, "That's not a good place to find a husband."

"Maybe, but there are no possibilities in our church."

"Trust God. He'll bring the man to you. I believe this."

Six months later, we were working at a church in Porto Alegre. We needed help cleaning the floor, so we asked the church in

Restinga to send helpers. Dude came. Unexpectedly, Gerimias, a man from a church in Porto Alegre, who had known us for years, also decided to help. We had not asked anyone from that church for assistance.

So, there we were, workers from three churches, cleaning the dried, thin layer of cement from the beautiful tile floor. I thought it was strange that Gerimias came to help us. He originally lived in Fortaleza, where we studied Portuguese. He was a very nice young man, someone who would make an excellent husband.

Around noon, I took him aside, "Do you have a girlfriend, you know, or someone whom you want to be your girlfriend, eventually?

"No, not yet."

"Take a look at the young lady from Restinga, over there cleaning tile. Do you see her?"

"Yeah, but she will not be interested in me."

"How do you know?" I could tell he was a bit shy and needed some encouragement to take the first step. "Just start chatting with her and let's see what the Lord might have in store for you two."

He did that. Later that night at my house, he was sitting next to Dude, with his arm around her shoulder. They hit it off well and soon were married. They went to Baptist Mid-Missions Bible College in Curitiba.

Ernesto and Luzia moved to São Paulo and remain in the ministry. Ten years later, Gerimias became the pastor of the church in Restinga and is still there.

In the spring of 1989, we went to the United States for a fifteen-month furlough. There, the boys could start studying at Pillsbury Baptist Bible College. Penny could also finish her degree.

*Dude (L) and Gerimias (R) are still working in our second church. I sometimes visit them in Restinga and preach there.*

*BAPTIZING LUZIA*

# CHAPTER 22

## Three Lathams at Pillsbury

Bob Anderson, a deacon at Bryant Avenue Baptist Church in Minneapolis, Minnesota, provided all the Accelerated Christian Education (ACE) curriculum materials we needed for our children. I moved Shane ahead in his studies so he could finish high school alongside Thomas. My plan was for both boys to complete their last year of high school together and begin as freshmen at Pillsbury College at the same time.

However, Thomas had other plans. He said, "I want to spend the summer living with the Ellsworths, in Minneapolis, and find a job. I can make enough to pay my own round-trip passage." We supported his decision to leave Brazil. After two months, he asked if he could remain and graduate from Bryant's ACE school. We agreed to this change.

Soon, Shane wanted a change, too. He said, "During my senior year, I want to attend a school that has soccer and wrestling." We arranged for Quentin and Lana Freeburg, who had three children, to host Shane for the year. Their home was just a block from Woodcrest Baptist Church, one of our supporting churches in Minnesota.

Penny, Kosy, and I followed their activities with great interest. In March, we started our furlough. We planned to live in Owatonna so Penny could finish her education. We rented a five-bedroom house, one-half block from Pillsbury College.

I spoke at both of our sons' high school graduations. After that, Shane worked, and Thomas attended Army boot camp. Penny, Kosy, and I visited our supporting churches west of the Mississippi River. We asked Jodi Endicott, a friend's daughter, to go with us so Kosy would not have to sit in the back seat by herself.

Our last meeting was in Great Falls, Montana. When we returned to Owatonna, Penny got set up to start classes, while I went to Fort Benning, Georgia, to see Thomas graduate from boot camp.

After the ceremony, his drill sergeant put his hand on Thomas' shoulder and said to me, "Mr. Latham, your son is not only a good soldier; he's also an excellent Christian."

Another soldier piped up, "Hey, Sarge, I'm also a Christian."

The drill sergeant smirked, "I know a Christian when I see one. You're not a Christian, but Thomas certainly is." I felt sorry for the other soldier who had not impressed his drill sergeant, but I was busting my buttons about Thomas's Christian testimony.

Penny registered for classes as a sophomore. She planned to graduate in May. To do that, she had to finish ninety-two hours of academic credit. Thirty hours a year was considered a full load.

The reason Penny could take ninety-two credit hours in one year was her intelligence and resourcefulness. I haven't known anyone else who finished college in two years. Penny convinced two teachers to let her complete the required reading and take only the midterm and final exams, without attending classes.

Meanwhile, I managed the cooking, housecleaning, and laundry.

During school breaks, Penny and I reported to our churches in Minnesota, Wisconsin, and Michigan. Sometimes, I went alone.

When wrestling season began at Pillsbury College, Jim Hazewinkel asked me to be his assistant coach. Jim and his twin brother Dave were in the 1968 and 1972 Olympics. It was an honor to help Jim in any way I could.

*PILLSBURY BAPTIST BIBLE COLLEGE WRESTLING TEAM*
*BACK ROW RIGHT: JIM HAZEWINKEL, TOM LATHAM*
*FRONT ROW (SECOND FROM RIGHT): SHANE LATHAM*

We were having a great time. In his Army uniform, our son Thomas carried the American flag for Harvest Home at Pillsbury College. We were all so proud of him.

Thomas joined the wrestling team, but after an alumni meet, stepped down. He told us wrestling was not his thing. Kosy was extremely proud of her two brothers. Shane, our other son, played soccer and wrestled. Our family went to as many of his games and matches as we could.

Penny and I had to attend a conference in Lafayette, Indiana. We stopped at Maranatha Baptist Bible College in Watertown, Wisconsin, to watch Shane wrestle in a tournament. I asked him, "Do you see that opponent? He just punched your mom in the nose. Blood is running down her face. Now, get out there and pin him." I didn't get the huge video recorder turned on in time, because Shane pinned his opponent in EIGHT SECONDS. Sometimes, motivation is everything.

We left Watertown and headed to Lafayette. Penny was driving while I slept a bit. She was driving on the inside lane of a four-lane highway as we were leaving Milwaukee, Wisconsin. There was about ten inches of snow on the road. As the car started spinning, I woke up just in time to see us going backwards on the road. Three lanes of cars were coming straight at us!

Grabbing the wheel, I turned it sharply counterclockwise. There was no doubt the hand of God was also on the steering wheel. Fortunately, there was a guardrail. We hugged it until the cars passed, and we came to a complete stop. The hood had even flown up, blocking our sight.

I got out, surveyed the situation, and tied the hood down. We continued to our destination, thanking God for His quick and successful help. When we got back to Owatonna, the insurance company paid for repairing the car.

We used the repaired car as a down payment on two new, identical, blue Chevy Geo Metros. Parking them outside the house, we asked the boys to come out because we had a present for them. Thomas got the first choice. He took the blue one! This was the only help we gave them for their college years, besides living with us.

*1991 BLUE CHEVY GEO METRO*

Penny was the only Latham who graduated. She got the *Prolific Artist Award* for doing the most art projects during the year. Penny's mom came to the graduation, as did Karen, her sister. We were so proud of Penny. The college president told us never to tell anyone she took ninety-two hours in one year.

Penny, Kosy, and I packed our things to return to Brazil and start our third church.

*Thomas, Shane, and Luiz Higgie (from Uruguay) came for the summer to help us with the construction of our third church.*

# CHAPTER 23

# Our Third Church

We wanted to start a church in Cachoeirinha, a city of 250,000 inhabitants. This city didn't have a church in our state association. After looking around for a while, we found a house with a large backyard. Since the house was only $7,000, we bought it. We planned to use the house as a parsonage, and then build the church at the back of the property.

We hired the mayor's construction company to build the church. Once the first floor was complete, Thomas, Shane and Luis Higgie (from Uruguay), arrived for the summer to help us. To prevent theft, I spent nights at the construction site until a Brazilian agreed to stay in my place.

We finished enough of the church construction to start services. Tony and Ana Paula were two of our first visitors. I set a time to teach them from my book for new converts. When we finished the first three chapters, they accepted Christ. After completing the course, we baptized them, and they began attending church, without missing a service.

One Sunday morning, Ana Paula came to church alone. "Is Tony sick?" I asked.

She looked at the ground and replied, "Not really. He has no decent shoes to wear in this cold weather."

I wanted to give her money to buy shoes, but before I could say a word, she handed me an envelope and said, "This is our first tithe."

I wanted to give the money back to her and tell her to buy shoes, so Tony could come to church. I didn't. Maybe that same generous and loving God I served could also meet their needs; I should give Him a chance to do so.

Tony came to the next service. Looking at his feet, I smiled. "Nice shoes, Tony."

"Can I say a word in church?" Tony asked.

I called on him at the end of the service. Tony is a humble person, which is rare to find these days.

He started his story. "As you all know, my mother died this week. None of the family had any money to pay for the burial. I asked my boss to fire me so I could use my severance money to pay the expenses. My boss said, 'No, I can't let you go, Tony, because you're my best worker. What's the cost of the burial?' I told him it was R$800 (about $200). He said he would pay for it. Listen to this: I've been a tither only for a week, and God gave me back five times what I gave Him." This is what I call my 'Tony the Tither' story.

Before we left our first church in Mossoró, we called Jose Bezerra to be the pastor. He had been a teenager at a church across town when we reopened our church. Jose worked at our Mossoró church for 13 years, earning a reputation as the humblest and most spiritual pastor in the state.

Jose wrote us a letter, expressing his love for our family and his desire to join us in the south. Though we were not ready to support a full-time pastor, we welcomed him, his wife Lucia, their three children, and a niece.

About this time, Kosy told us she wanted to finish her secondary education at Owatonna High School. She went to Minnesota on her own and began living with the Dennis Sleen family, who went to Grace Baptist Church in Owatonna. Grace Baptist was one of our supporting churches.

Penny and I went on furlough early enough to attend Shane and Erin's wedding in Belgrade, Montana. After the ceremony, I escaped with Erin in Shane's car, meeting him on the service road by the freeway. Still in her wedding dress, Erin got out, climbed through the barbed wire fence, and took off with Shane in another car. This was to avoid any tomfoolery by the attendees. Shane and Erin went to Brazil for their honeymoon, staying in our house in Porto Alegre.

*This was our home in Porto Alegre where we lived alone when all the children were in the USA.*

Before we left for furlough, we painted our church's information on the wall of a four-story building. This was one of the best advertising ideas we ever had. A Christian couple, Paulo and Núbia Rodrigues, saw the sign and started coming to the services.

When we were on furlough, I spent a lot of time on the phone, arranging forty deputation meetings for Shane and Erin along the U.S. East Coast. We drove our son Tom's Geo Metro to Miami, leaving it there for Shane and Erin to use on deputation.

OUR THIRD CHURCH IN CACHOEIRINHA

*I'm baptizing Leila, a German lady, in our third church.*

# CHAPTER 24

## Are You Kidding Me?

In 1985, I was visiting my mom in Battle Ground, Washington, when she said, "I want to tell you this before I die: Harry Latham is not your biological father."

I was dumbfounded, to say the least. "What?!"

"Yes. He's also not Harriet's father, either. Her father was an Apache Indian; your father is Carl Orr, from the Cherokee Tribe."

Harry Latham left us when I was two years old. I saw him a few times after that, once with Penny and the kids. He never told me he wasn't my biological father, and maybe he never knew. I was shocked by the news, but not unhappy. I wondered if Carl Orr, my birth father, might be a good man—possibly rich or talented. I was disappointed on all counts.

After learning the truth, I decided to look for Carl Orr. I called the operator in Newark, Ohio, where Mom said he lived, and asked for his number. She couldn't find it. When I requested numbers for all the Orrs listed, she said that wasn't allowed. I then politely asked for her supervisor.

I told the supervisor I was trying to find my biological father. She immediately gave me five Orr phone numbers. I called the first two; neither knew a Carl. On my third call, a woman answered:

"Yeah, I know Carl. I'm his aunt. He doesn't live in Newark but in Zanesville." She gave me his number.

This is where Dale Carnegie's advice from his book, *How to Win Friends and Influence People*, comes in handy. He suggests getting people to say 'Yes' as often as possible so they're more likely to say 'YES' when you ask for something important.

The call went like this:

"Is this Carl Orr?"

"Yes." (1)

"Are you B.J. Orr's son?"

"Yes." (2)

"Did your dad have a girlfriend in Newark?"

"Yes." (3)

"Did you ever go to Newark with your dad when he went to see Old Ma Latham, as they called her?"

"Yes." (4)

"In July of 1944, did you go there with your dad and meet a young lady by the name of Loretta Latham?"

"Yes." (5) "Why are you asking me these questions?"

*(We must leave Dale Carnegie's theory now.)*

"It's because I'm Tommy Latham and my mother, Loretta Latham, told me you're my biological dad."

"How old are you?" he asked.

"I'm forty years old."

"Well, you can't be my son, because I have a daughter who's forty."

"Oh, give me a break, will you? Are you saying I'm not your son? Okay. I'll have another talk with Mom." And, before Arnold Schwarzenegger made the phrase popular, I said, "I'll be back."

When I talked to Mom, she said, "Ask him this: Did you come to Albany, Oregon, in 1949 to see me? When you asked Mom if I was your son, did she say 'Yes'?"

Three days later, I called him and said, "I'm baaaack!" I asked him the new questions Mom gave me. This time, he admitted he was my biological dad.

I traveled to Zanesville to meet Carl Orr. He wasn't very excited to see me. He already had three children: Bonnie (who was my age), Kimberly, and Gary.

I got their addresses and wrote letters of introduction. Bonnie, the oldest, was the leader. Things went well with Bonnie for a while. Then, because of some confusion in our conversations, our correspondence was put on hold.

Six years later, I was in Colorado. Bonnie lives in a suburb of Denver. I knocked on her door. She was visiting Kim in San Francisco. I was still on hold.

Two years after that, I wrote to Bonnie again. I explained that she and Kim were my only sisters. I also told them my other sister, Harriet, was killed by the Mafia when she was twenty-nine. I explained to her that if she allowed me to visit, I would really appreciate it.

She did let me visit her. Her husband died shortly afterward. Bonnie then married Tony, a retired military man. For more than twenty-five years, Bonnie and I have been very close. She has flown to three places where Penny and I were in the States, to visit us.

Tony and Bonnie paid for three days at a hotel in Rapid City, South Dakota, so we could spend time together. Tony recently died, so Bonnie and I are in the same boat now, trying to cope with horrendous losses. Hers was a double loss.

After talking to Bonnie the first time, I went to San Francisco and told Kim about my life before I was a Christian. She said, "Wow! Men with backgrounds like that sometimes turn out to be serial killers."

"You're right. Now I'm going to give you the rest of the story."

After I told her about my becoming a follower of Jesus, she said, "You're a fanatic."

"I know I am, and the name fits me fine."

I hadn't met Gary, because we don't go through Reno, where he lives. Eight years later, Kim wrote me a letter saying, "Tommy, I think you might like to hear this. I went to Reno to visit our brother, Gary. He took me to a Baptist church, and I got saved. Now, I'm a fanatic just like you!"

We've been together several times. One time was at Thanksgiving in Colorado Springs, Colorado, where I first met Gary. My siblings love me dearly, and I love them.

*I enjoyed visiting my biological sisters,*
*Bonnie (L) and Kimberly (R).*

*I'm with Gary (L), my brother, and Tony, Bonnie's husband.*

> *"But I say unto you which hear, Love your enemies, do good to them which hate you, Bless them that curse you, and pray for them which despitefully use you.*
>
> *"And unto him that smiteth thee on the one cheek offer also the other; and him that taketh away thy cloak forbid not to take thy coat also.*
>
> *"Give to every man that asketh of thee; and of him that taketh away thy goods ask them not again."*
>
> *Luke 6:27-30*

*ME WITH MY 1951 FORD*

# CHAPTER 25

## Revenge is Biblical

In 1995, Penny and I were living alone in Porto Alegre, still working at the church we had started in Cachoeirinha. Our son, Thomas, was serving in the Army, Shane was attending Pillsbury Baptist Bible College in Minnesota, and Kosy was staying with the Sleen family in Owatonna while going to high school.

Because Penny knew my love of antique cars, she encouraged me to purchase a 1951 Ford she spotted during one of our drives around the city. This was our second venture into classic car ownership. We bought it for $1,000 and found it needed an oil change.

ME WITH MY 1951 CHEVY

This was different from when we owned the '51 Chevy, which had been our only car for two years. Now, with the '51 Ford, we also owned a 1995 VW Golf. The Chevy had a perfect body but a poor motor and steering. The steering wheel would turn to the right if you let go of it. In contrast, the Ford had a worn body but a strong V-8 flathead motor.

I could put sixteen kids in this Ford. We did that a few times, too. I taught them how to do a Chinese fire drill at a red light. We made a mistake in doing it when a policeman was watching. He didn't appreciate American culture; I got a ticket for being reckless.

Later, when we moved to Gravataí, we took the Ford with us. We still had it when several U.S. groups visited. Penny didn't enjoy the rides; the motor's fumes always seeped into the passenger area.

Conflict with a young man in our third church stood out: he openly insulted me for not allowing rock music in our services and for refusing to let Mormons come into our building. He called me a jerk in front of everyone.

The following Monday morning, I went to his house and knocked on the door. He opened it, expecting me to chew him out. "May I sit down?" I asked. He reluctantly let me do so.

I slid the Ford title toward him. "I know it's hard for your family to get to church when it rains, having to take two buses. I'm giving you this '51 Ford. I suggest you sell it while it's still running. Use the money to buy a car that will be less expensive to repair." Then, I got up and walked out.

In the next church service, he asked to say something. "My sister raised me because I never had a dad. Pastor Thomas loved this Ford. It means a lot that he gave it to me. I want to thank him publicly for it." Since that day, this young man has treated me as if I were his father. That biblical form of revenge cost me $1,000.

Another incident took place when I was remodeling a different church in Porto Alegre. We let a young man live in the building because he was helping me with the renovations. He began stealing from the church—a fan disappeared first, then some church documents.

After investigating the matter, I discovered he had gone to the city and asked for some other documents. He had Xeroxed his name as the property owner and was trying to sell it to the neighbors. When I confronted him about it, he said, "Yeah, I own this place now, but you can preach here until I sell it."

As I tried to leave and get help, the young man grabbed me and pinned me to the wall. Despite his appearance—he was very skinny, and his arms looked weak—he seemed unusually strong at that moment. It felt like I was being overpowered by an enemy of God.

Breaking loose, I found a policeman on the street. He said he didn't want to get involved. Eventually, other police officers arrived. I explained the situation to them. One officer said, "By law, we can't throw him out of his living quarters, but we see what's going on here."

He looked at the kid and said, "You have ten minutes to put the church documents in the pastor's hand. If you don't, we're going to take you downtown to headquarters. There, I predict, you'll accidentally fall down the stairs. Do you get my drift?"

He said he did understand and returned the documents. They also told him to get his things and hit the road. A man living next door to the church found out what had happened. He stopped me the next day and told me what a horrible person I was. I didn't know how to respond, so I said nothing and left.

After going home, I made cinnamon rolls and took them to my neighbor's door at eight o'clock the next morning. He didn't want them. I shoved my arm past the door and said, "Take them. I don't know why we can't be friends." He took them.

A week later, when his car wouldn't start, I helped him push it without saying anything. A month after that, Penny and I saw him at an opera intermission. He saw us, called out my name, and motioned for us to come over. He put his hand on my shoulder and introduced me to others: "This is Pastor Thomas, my American friend."

After all, the Bible does say to 'heap hot cinnamon rolls on their head,' right?

Here's another story of how revenge worked out: A neighbor had been harassing me and causing us a lot of anguish and sleepless nights. One day, when he was not so mean, he visited us, right after I had made cinnamon rolls. I didn't eat any because I noticed some bugs in the rolls, their feet pointing to heaven. Apparently, the bugs were in the old flour.

When he saw the rolls, he asked if he could take some home. I let him take the whole batch, claiming I could make some more.

# CHAPTER 26

## We've Been Robbed—Again!

The first time our family was robbed was when someone at the storehouse in Fortaleza used a hacksaw to cut open our metal barrel and stole a tape recorder and my Marty Robbins *Gunfighter Ballads*, a 78rpm record.

By December 2023, we had been robbed 114 times. Here, I will share the stories about five of those robberies. In three of the stories, the robber pointed a gun at my head.

**Robbery One**

One Sunday after church, someone from our congregation took Penny home. I stayed behind to drive the other members home in our 12-passenger van. When I finally got home, I pulled into the garage and went back to close the gate, locking it as I always did.

When I got to the porch, two teens with hoodies came around the corner and pointed a gun at my head, saying, "Don't say a word or we'll kill you."

What they wanted me to do was to fall on my knees and beg for mercy. They planned to make me open the locked door; then they would enter the house and put the gun to Penny's head. They would gather everything of value, put it in our van, and drive away.

That was never going to happen! I would have fought them to the death before I would have allowed them to put a gun to Penny's head. I knew that the front door was locked. Penny had heard what they said, so she ran to get my air rifle. She was not going to open the door.

I said, "I don't think you're going to rob me, because my neighbor has a shotgun." I ran to the gate and screamed, "Nelson, Nelson, I'm being robbed." (He's my friend across the road who has several weapons.)

Nelson came out with his gun. Three other neighbors also ran outside, shouting. The thieves, startled by this response, ran to the back of our property and disappeared into the woods. My reaction clearly unsettled them.

## Robbery Two

The next day, I bought a pellet gun that closely resembled a real firearm. That evening, I had it in my car as we arrived home after dark. I got out to open the gate and was suddenly confronted by a large man. He was holding a gun and aimed a shaking hand at me. He stammered, "This ... This ... is ... a ... robbery." He appeared even more frightened than I was.

I screamed again, "Nelson, Nelson, robbery!" My neighbor came out, blasting his shotgun into the air. Other neighbors burst through their doors, brooms in hand.

The robber fled down the road toward a waiting car. I grabbed my air pistol and chased him, but I didn't shoot because I couldn't locate the safety button.

I believe the robber was terrified because he saw my guardian angel, with his sword drawn; maybe the angel was saying, "Not today." I don't have to see the angel to believe I have one. "Are not all angels ministering spirits sent to serve those who will inherit salvation?" (*Hebrews 1:14*)

## Robbery Three

One night while we were in bed, Penny said, "There's someone on the roof."

I didn't hear anything because I wasn't wearing my hearing aids. I told Penny, "It's probably a cat."

"No, this is bigger than a cat."

Soon after, our house alarm began blaring. I went upstairs but found nothing. After resetting the alarm and returning to bed, it sounded again. I checked upstairs a second time but still saw no one. Ten minutes later, the alarm went off for a third time.

This time, I grabbed a pointed stick—something we use at the top of the stairs to keep the sliding door closed. Stepping into the hallway, I saw a small person standing at the entrance to the bedrooms. He said, "I've passed this house many times, and I've always wanted to see what it looked like on the inside."

"Hey, right! Do you have a gun?" I asked.

"No, and you are lucky I don't."

"You think so? Well, kid, let me tell you this: You're lucky I don't have a gun. If I shot you, your soul would go down to hell. If you shot me, my soul would go up to heaven."

By this time, Penny had already called the police. She was waiting outside with our neighbors. The neighbors didn't want to enter the house because they feared the robber might recognize their faces and return for revenge.

The kid was holding a book he had stolen from one of the bedrooms. It was Tim Lahaye's *Left Behind*. "This book looks interesting," he said, "but I can't read English."

"That's because you don't care to study; you just want to rob people. Look at the flames of hell on the front cover. That's where you're going to go when you die." Frankly, this is not my most enjoyable way to witness.

The police finally came. "Sorry, Tom, you know how it is. This city has 100 policemen on the streets during the day, but only two at night. What do you have here?"

"The kid is in the room to the left."

"Do you mind if we rough him up a bit?"

"No, because he'll be walking out the front door at the police station while I'm still filling out paperwork."

I heard some noise from the room, and soon after, the kid was brought out in handcuffs. Later, at the police station, I was still filling out paperwork when I saw the robber walk right past me and leave through the front door.

"Hey, why's the kid leaving, the one who just invaded my home?"

"He's a minor. Also, he didn't rob you, didn't have a gun or a knife, and didn't harm you. So, he walks," the policeman explained.

I asked to talk to the chief of police; it was 2 AM. The officer called the chief. I always say, when talking on the phone, "Excuse my Portuguese, I'm not Brazilian." When I said this, he hung up on me, knowing I couldn't vote in Brazil.

## Robbery Four

I was at a bank that was five blocks from our church. I took out R$6.000 (about $1,500) to pay workers. When I got to the church, I called out to our deacon, Paulo, to come and get his money. Foolishly, I was holding it out the window as I sat in the car.

Before Paulo could get there, a young man jumped off the back of a motorcycle, ran around the car, and grabbed the money from my hand. He put a gun to my temple and said, "Give me the rest of it."

I struggled with him while trying to keep my documents. He pistol-whipped me and grabbed the rest of the money from my wallet. Paulo wanted to intervene, but felt if he did, the kid would have killed me, and maybe others, too. He was probably right.

The robber got on the motorcycle and zoomed away. Evidently, someone at the bank had seen me withdrawing money and tipped off an accomplice, telling him the man in the orange jacket had taken out six thousand reais and should be followed. That explains why, after grabbing the R$1.500,00 in my hand, the robber also demanded the remaining R$4.500,00. Unfortunately, the pistol whipping broke a nerve in my neck and caused pain for a couple of years.

## Robbery Five

Now for a major robbery: the wife of Kosy's pastor arrived from the USA before Kosy did. She came to do a women's conference at our church. We took her to Gramado for a few hours. While we were gone, our daughter Kosy arrived from the USA. She called me and said, "Dad, something's wrong. The front gate and the front door were open! I think you've been robbed."

"Is Mom's red car in the driveway?"

"No."

"Is my Harley Davidson there?"

"No. Dad, the house is a mess, and all your computers and household appliances are gone."

The thieves took over $40,000 worth of our personal property. Neighbors, seeing what was happening, assumed we were moving rather than being robbed.

About three weeks later, the robber called me to see if I wanted to buy the Harley back. They discovered that selling its parts was not going to happen, because Harley owners will not buy stolen parts. They are a close-knit club.

I said, "You can get on the Harley and ride it to the abyss, because that's where you and your friends are all going."

"What a horrible pastor you are, condemning us to hell."

"I'm not doing that. You're doing it to yourself, by your own wicked choices."

"If you don't buy it back, we're going to cut it to pieces with a blow torch."

"Go ahead. I have insurance."

If I had taken the cash to them, they would have killed me, taken the money, and still have kept my bike. A week later, he called again to see if I had changed my mind. I hadn't. A year later, the police found where the robbers stored their stolen things. The Harley was there, not damaged.

~~~~~~~~~~~~~~~~~~~~~~~~~~~~~~~~~~~~~~~~~~~~~~~~~~

Why do we remain in Brazil after 114 robberies? We are committed to loving and serving the Brazilians, who have suffered this violence, too. Our janitor, for example, was robbed and shot. God has not told us to leave, so we stay and do our best to prevent more robberies.

I've suffered from what I call MPTSD (Missionary Post Traumatic Stress Disorder). Sometimes I have bad dreams. I wake up screaming, sweating, or thinking someone is breaking into my bedroom. It's not a pleasant experience.

~~~~~~~~~~~~~~~~~~~~~~~~~~~~~~~~~~~~~~~~~~~~~~~~~~

> If through a broken heart God can bring His purposes to pass in the world, then thank Him for breaking your heart.

*At the Harley store, this was the only motorcycle they had in the showroom. I joined the elite club of Harley owners. I eventually sold the bike so Penny could have surgery.*

*This is the sign Paulo and Núbia saw and came to our new church.*

# CHAPTER 27

# The Sign That Flew

I believed that, in our city of 250,000, at least 1,000 people would attend our church if only they knew it existed. Our building was just a block off the main road, but no one passing by would recognize that a Baptist church was so close.

When Paulo and Núbia noticed the first painted sign on a nearby four-story building, we saw how even one sign could bring new people to our church. Encouraged by this, we decided to see if another sign would attract even more visitors.

I designed a sign measuring five by ten feet. It displayed our church's name and a large arrow pointing toward the church. After obtaining the apartment owner's permission, we were going to place it on the side of the building, across the street from the first sign.

As we began putting up the heavy sign, we noticed the wind was picking up. Six men used ropes to pull the sign up the side of the building. When it reached the roof, Thomas Settell, a teenager from Bryant Avenue Christian Day School, who was helping us, said, "This wind is too strong. We can't hang it over the side right now."

We left the sign on the roof and set it down. For some reason, I put a small brick under it. Thomas warned, "You can't leave that brick under the sign. The wind might get under it, blowing it off the roof."

I replied that the wind couldn't possibly be that strong, since the sign was behind a three-foot wall. "The wind would have to blow it over this wall. I don't think that's possible."

We decided to leave the sign on the roof and return to the church to wait for the wind to subside. About three hours later, someone ran in and shouted, "The sign went flying! The sign went flying!"

We hurried to the street, where we found our sign smashed into a tree. The wind had lifted it, carried it over the three-foot wall, floated it above the neighboring building, and crashed it into a tree. We were astonished. The sign truly had flown.

The sign could have caused serious harm if it had landed differently. It could have hit a car or truck driving by on the street. Worse yet, it might have hit a person on the street and killed them. We were grateful that no damage occurred, and we felt that God had protected everyone involved.

We cut the sign in half and placed one part on the church building. We asked the apartment owner again about putting the smaller sign on the side of the building he was responsible for.

He said, "Some of the apartment owners don't want the sign. It says 'Baptist Church' on it. They're not Baptist. To them, it's the same thing as putting up a political sign for the party of which they are not a member."

# CHAPTER 28

# Gigi and Fernanda

I gave a Chick tract to a policeman during carnival weekend. Later, he came to church and said, "I'm already a believer, but my boss really needs this message. Can you go with me to his house?"

I agreed to go. The house was full of people, but Sergeant Vando Araujo, the policeman's boss, was not interested in the gospel. While there, I noticed his eleven-year-old daughter, Gigi, sitting on the floor with a cast up past her knee—she'd just been hit by a car. She looked up at me and asked, "You're an American, aren't you?"

"Yes."

Gigi began singing a song from the Titanic movie. I was amazed when she started singing in English. I asked, "Do you want to study English?" She said she did. I set it up; I would go to her house for one hour a week. She would have to study two hours a day, or I would not come back.

Gigi accepted the challenge. She didn't pay for the classes, though an American teaching English in Brazil typically earns $15 per hour. Her talent for languages was evident. Her progress was phenomenal—within a few months, she could understand and say simple phrases like, "See you later, alligator."

Using my book for new converts, I taught Gigi, her mother Inez, and her brother Gabriel. Gigi's dad was not interested. Gigi, Inez, and Gabriel soon accepted Christ. Gigi joined our youth group and the drama team at our third church. Her home life was difficult, mainly due to her father.

Penny and I went to Gigi's high school graduation. Her exceptional English skills opened opportunities after graduation. She worked at a local clinic while training to be a nurse, and ultimately got a job in administration on a Florida-based cruise ship.

Penny and I took a cruise to see her. But she had been transferred to another ship. She left us a Christmas gift and a note.

*"I owe you the best years of my childhood. Thank you for introducing me to Jesus, and for being there when I needed you the most. I love you both with all my heart."* ♥ *Gigi*

Gigi stopped by my office in 2023 to tell us she had gotten a job as a hotel manager near us in Gramado. She was close by for a while, but eventually went back to the cruise ship.

Although Gigi's dad was not interested in the gospel, he said his boss needed it. He took me to see his boss.

When I opened the door, I immediately saw a broken teenager. Fernanda was fourteen years old, the daughter of the chief of police. He was not interested in the gospel. She had considered suicide several times due to serious family problems.

I gave Fernanda the same offer as Gigi. Fernanda's ability to learn English was remarkable. I began leading her family in a study of my book for new converts. Eventually, Fernanda and her family accepted Christ, although her dad did not—yet.

Fernanda joined our drama team, too. She was a delight—happy, smiling, helpful, respectful, and growing spiritually. Having both girls in our youth group was a pleasure. Penny supported me with them and provided much-needed counseling, even helping their mothers.

We took six teens from our drama team to Uruguay; Fernanda was one of them. Even though she didn't speak Spanish, she got the 'Camper of the Week' award. She kept studying and was very good at speaking English with hardly any accent.

I arranged with Bryant Avenue Baptist Church in Minneapolis, Minnesota, to have her accepted into their Accelerated Christian Education school, from which she graduated. We got to the U.S. just after that and spent some time with her before she went back to Brazil.

Fernanda now has two lovely daughters, Hannah and Alice, both of whom follow Jesus and work as professional models. I baptized Hannah. Stories like Fernanda's and Gigi's are what kept us on the mission field, despite many trials.

*Our fourth, and most likely final, location in Brazil was the city of Gravataí in the state of Rio Grande do Sul.*

*Tom and Pat Sheldon have been very generous to us all during our missionary ministry.*

# CHAPTER 29

## Moving to Gravataí

Every Sunday, we drove three hours from Porto Alegre to our third church in Cachoeirinha. Deciding to settle closer, we bought an empty lot just 900 feet from the main highway to the mountain tourist cities. This spot offered easy bus access and a short walk for visitors.

During construction in March 1995, my brother Danny sent me a letter with only one sentence: "Tommy, before I die, I want you to know that I found God." He passed away soon after. I still wonder about its meaning. Before my wife died in 2023, I asked her: "Penny, after you see Jesus, then your dad and sister, look for my Grandfather Taylor. He made a spiritual decision at church two weeks before he passed away. Then, look for my brother Danny." She agreed.

We listed our Porto Alegre house for sale while I started building our new home, hoping to move soon. Selling took three years, but in June 1996, we moved to our partly finished house in Gravataí.

Following the moving truck, we arrived at the new house at 2 AM—with no front door installed. Penny and I slept on a mattress in the living room as stray dogs wandered by. The next day, we secured the front door, but our bedroom still had no windows installed. That night, cats climbed in and out through the gaps in the wall. Penny did not appreciate the feline presence.

We employed 15 men to finish the downstairs so we could move in and start our new life. Over time, we bought two more lots, creating a soccer field, volleyball court, and bocce-ball court.

A year later, we completed the second floor as a retreat center with 26 beds, three bathrooms, and a large game room. I made two of the games in the room. The space hosted many retreats and overnighters, including one where eighty women attended a chocolate retreat, with some sleeping upstairs and others camping outside.

I built a two-story playground, 8 feet wide by 78 feet long, filled with equipment to attract children and public schools to our property. One day, we hosted 200 students from a public school. I shared my salvation story and distributed Chick tracts.

As missionaries, Penny and I understood our work was a lifelong commitment. My doctoral thesis, *Missionary Problem Areas*, examined six main reasons missionaries quit and return home.

During fifty years of ministry, we faced seven major crises, any of which could have led us to quit. Fellow believers and missionaries caused most of them.

We endured these challenges by never blaming God for the faults of His followers. We understood that people acted carnally due to Satan, not God. Satan opposes God's work of saving souls.

Another key to staying on the mission field was embracing the country, even though its language, customs, and thinking were unfamiliar. We admired James Hudson Taylor, who adopted local Chinese dress as a missionary.

Speaking Portuguese with an American accent was sometimes

embarrassing or funny, but it never stopped me from taking advantage of the opportunities God provided. In fact, Brazilians were often interested in hearing my accent, which drew their attention—just as I enjoy different English accents.

FOURTH CHURCH
GRAVATAÍ, RIO GRANDE DO SUL, BRAZIL

OUR HOME IN GRAVATAÍ (HOSTING 200)

*Would you like a donut right now?*

*Clerks at a downtown store enjoyed sweet rolls.*

# CHAPTER 30

# Donut Ministry

Many of our greatest ministries and family projects began as Penny's ideas. Her creativity shone as she'd say, "I have an idea. You need to listen to the whole plan before you give me an answer." I always tried to hear her out, and to her credit, I said "Yes" more often than "No."

I enjoyed making cinnamon rolls, and one day, I made too many. Penny suggested taking the extra rolls to the teachers at the public school near our house. When I delivered them, the teachers asked why I brought treats. I replied, "A public school teacher really must love children to do this job. I know how little you make, and if I were president of this country, I would triple your salary."

They wanted to know if I could run for president. "I can't even vote," I answered. "You teachers deserve a lot of respect and all the perks imaginable!"

Inspired by their response, I decided to reach out to other public schools in our city. I called various schools to find out the times of their coffee breaks during the morning and afternoon sessions.

I always arrived early, finding a seat before the teachers came in for their break. They were surprised by the beautiful, fragrant rolls, especially the ones with prunes and walnuts. I spent time chatting with the teachers, listening to their stories, and sharing my testimony.

Next, I considered taking cinnamon rolls to the police station and the fire hall. The firemen welcomed me warmly. The police seemed less appreciative; perhaps they were suspicious and thought I was seeking future favors. As a result, I stopped taking rolls to the police station.

The firemen showed their appreciation by turning on their siren whenever they passed our house, hinting at more rolls. One day, as I was driving near home, a fire truck with flashing lights and a blaring siren pulled me over, and a fireman leaned in to ask, "Pastor Thomas, when are you going to bring us more donuts?"

I also took donuts to the stores downtown. After a few deliveries, I invited the store workers to our house for shish kebabs. During their visit, I shared my testimony of salvation. When summer came, and school was out, I took cinnamon rolls to gas stations and continued inviting people to our home.

Eventually, I decided to ask the public schools if I could start wrestling practice. Since they already trusted me, because of the sweet rolls, they agreed. The cinnamon rolls had opened doors for us!

One day, I entered a teacher's lounge with donuts, hoping to get permission to start a wrestling team. The director from another school, where I already had a team, recognized me and asked, "Pastor Thomas, what are you doing here?"

"I brought these donuts for the teachers. What are you doing here?"

She replied, "Well, you know how much we make. I have to teach here in the afternoon to pay my bills." Turning to the other teachers, she announced, "Listen up, teachers, Pastor Thomas is going to tell you his life story."

I thought this was amazing. Here was an unsaved school principal asking me to give my Christian testimony to her unsaved coworkers!

This donut ministry probably wouldn't work in the United States, where Dunkin' Donuts stores are everywhere, and their donuts are cheap and delicious. At the time I was making rolls and donuts, no place in our twin cities of 500,000 people (about half the population of South Dakota) sold donuts.

*I made cream-filled donuts with chocolate frosting and whipped cream. I was privileged to bake and give away the only donuts in our town, with a population of 250,000.*

*The referee is ready to raise my arm after I pinned another opponent during a Pillsbury Baptist Bible College wrestling match. (I won "Most Pins" each year.)*

2012 STATE WRESTLING CHAMPIONS

# CHAPTER 31

## Freestyle Wrestling Ministry

My passions have been in this order:
    1) Christ,
    2) Penny,
    3) family,
    4) ministry, and
    5) freestyle wrestling.

I loved my wrestling years at Pillsbury Baptist Bible College, where Penny was my most avid fan. Our team won the conference title every year.

I had always wanted to start a wrestling ministry in Brazil, but the standard three-piece mat was too expensive and too heavy to move. Then, at an event, Penny and I saw a mat made of smaller three-foot-by-six-foot sections that fit together like a puzzle.

Seeing the puzzle mat made us realize a wrestling ministry was possible. I ordered fifty sections for $3,000 and had a trailer built to carry the mat behind our van. We packed the mat sections inside and made space in front for a bag of singlets. (A singlet is a wrestler's uniform.) Our van also helped us transport

wrestlers and assistant coaches.

We got permission to wrestle at the public school, but we could only do it at 5:00 PM, after school was out, and the students were going home. To participate, the students had to stay until 6:00 PM.

Each time we started, about forty to fifty students joined. Over time, this number dropped to only five to eight wrestlers. We couldn't continue with so few participants, so we moved to new schools when needed. Thankfully, we had enough schools to keep the program running for twenty years.

At one point, we held wrestling in schools every Monday, Tuesday, Wednesday, and Friday. At first, only boys participated. I didn't have singlets yet, so I asked a neighbor to sew uniforms using the Minnesota Gophers' colors, maroon and gold.

When I advertised in *Amateur Wrestling News* for donations of wrestling singlets, I received them from all over the USA. We ended up with over three hundred singlets, including some from the high school in Owatonna, Minnesota.

On tournament Saturdays, I would rent a bus to stop at all four schools, pick up students, and take them to the church. We had huge turnouts, including wrestlers from five other teams in our state. Some great wrestlers, who had competed in tournaments in Rio de Janeiro, gave our program credibility.

In twenty years, we went to eighteen public schools. Finally, Geronimo, a school only three blocks from the church, allowed us to train during school hours. We would pick up helpers and arrive at the school at 3:00 PM.

After laying out the mat, students from second through third grade came from 3:30 to 4:00 PM. Next, the fourth through sixth graders came from 4:00 to 4:30 PM. We held a school tournament every month.

We had to organize tournaments for 120 wrestlers in just one hour so we could finish before recess. Careful planning made this possible. After three years, a new principal ended our program, so we moved practices to the church on Saturday mornings.

A few years later, two public schools allowed us to wrestle during school hours. We went to one school on Tuesday and the other school on Wednesday. I took donuts to the teachers and workers at every practice. We had a tournament at the church every third Saturday.

I trained 120 students at the two schools and at our church. Only 10 wrestlers from the two public schools were attending tournaments. I paid Uber drivers to bring the wrestlers to our Saturday practice and the tournaments. I usually paid about 4 Uber drivers, but was willing to pay for many more. Unfortunately, few parents had enough interest in their children to bring them to practice or to the tournaments.

Back in 2012, I took ten boys and girls to the state championship tournament in Porto Alegre. We won first place. Since the medals they gave us were just plastic and had nothing written on them, I made a special medal for them.

The wrestling ministry became much more than a sport; it was a way to connect with and positively influence our community. At one point, one-third of our congregation came from this outreach. This shows how deeply the wrestling program impacted lives.

Looking back over fifty years of missionary work, I remain committed to serving as long as I am able. I hope to continue mentoring youth through wrestling and ministry, and maybe someday become recognized as the oldest youth pastor or wrestling coach.

In 2019, I had three stents put in my heart. The doctor said I have the heart of an eighteen-year-old, but the rest of my body hasn't figured it out yet!

*I had three national champions and a second placer; this gave us the 2010 Brazilian National Championship. We had only one chance to win, and we did it.*

# CHAPTER 32

## Andressa, Larissa, and Carla

After a few months in a boys' program, Isadora and Isabelle, twin sisters, asked me if they could wrestle. "No, my program is just for boys," I answered.

After Penny and I talked it over, we decided to include girls in the program. Two of our churches dropped our support because of this decision. They believed it was a sin for women to wear pants, let alone a wrestling singlet. Still, we felt including girls was the right decision.

Our first supporting church was also considering dropping us, but they gave me a chance to explain. I told them many of the girls came to school wearing tank tops that showed their belly buttons or very short pants, and the singlet was actually more modest. This church understood my reasoning and decided not to drop us.

Andressa became the best female wrestler I had, so I asked her to be the girls' coach. She lived a few blocks from our house and would help me attach the trailer to the van before we headed out. Andressa's dad died when she was nine years old, and her sister, Larissa, was just six months old. For the last ten years, I've been like an adopted dad to them.

When Andressa graduated from high school, I 'lost' her in a sense: She got a job and married one of the wrestlers. She once sent me this letter on Father's Day:

~~~~~~~~~~~~~~~~~~~~~~~~~~~~~~~~~~~~~~~~~~~~~~~~

*I couldn't forget to say Happy Father's Day to you. You'll always be my father and pastor. Today I love Christ because you planted the love of Christ in me, and I continue to cultivate that love.*

*That's what a father does, right? He teaches his children to love God above all things? You fulfilled this role for me.*

*Andressa, your daughter*

~~~~~~~~~~~~~~~~~~~~~~~~~~~~~~~~~~~~~~~~~~~~~~~~

After Andressa moved on, her sister Larissa took her place on the team. Larissa proved to be the toughest female wrestler I've ever had. She was small but fast and very strong.

In 2010, I took Larissa and three boys—Maurício, Leonardo, and Gabriel—to Rio de Janeiro for the first Brazilian Freestyle National Championship. Forty wrestlers were competing. Maurício and his brother Leonardo each pinned their only opponents, while Gabriel took second place.

When I was registering the wrestlers, the officials told me Larissa could not participate because she was only eleven, and the minimum age was twelve. I explained I hadn't known about the rule, or I wouldn't have brought her. I asked if they could be flexible since I had paid for her airfare and three days of lodging and food. I told them if they gave her a chance, she would show them what she could do.

The officials agreed, and Larissa was allowed to wrestle. She pinned three girls—aged 13, 14, and 15—who were all taller and heavier than she was. She completed this remarkable task in only two minutes total mat time and, at eleven years old, became a national champion.

Several years later, Larissa got married. She asked me to walk her down the aisle. I met her at the door. She put her arm in mine and said, "You will always be my father."

I teared up, feeling overwhelmed with pride and happiness. I replied, "And you, Princess, will always be my daughter."

Experiences like these don't happen to missionaries who quit. It takes decades to build such personal relationships. Penny and I spent five decades developing these bonds.

For more than fifteen years, Carla Menezes coached my girl wrestlers. She's a mother of eleven children. Her two sons, Maurício and Leonardo, were the ones who went to Rio with me in 2010 and both won national championships.

Carla is compassionate, and the children loved her. She had a special relationship with the wrestlers and handled any injuries during public school sessions or tournaments. In 2023, she brought her grandson to practices, sometimes leaving him with Cida, our church janitor, to watch while she coached.

Even though Carla was a grandmother of six, she still wrestled at some tournaments because we didn't always have competitors for the heavier weight classes. This was a fantastic feat that few women her age would even consider.

I could always count on a friendly smile and a helping hand from Carla. I expect she will continue in this endeavor for as long as we are allowed to do this essential and successful ministry.

*THREE GIRLS' WRESTLING COACHES*
*LARISSA (L), CARLA (C), AND ANDRESSA (R)*

# CHAPTER 33

## Getting a Van Driver's License

Faith Baptist Church of Lebanon, Pennsylvania, purchased a van for us. The van burned either gas or propane. To drive the van, I needed a bus driver's license, since Brazil requires one for any vehicle with more than nine seats.

In Brazil, if someone has a ticket on their record, they can't take the classes needed for a bus license. I was unable to take these classes because of one ticket. However, tickets are removed after one year, giving drivers a clean record.

Just before my ticket was about to be removed from my record, I got another one. This meant I needed to wait a whole year before taking the test. As long as I avoided new tickets for the next 365 days, I could take the test after that period.

Frustrated by the situation, I decided to take action. I wrote a letter to the Department of Motor Vehicles explaining my need for the van in my roles as a youth pastor and wrestling coach for the community. They responded by asking me to call them. Before calling, I prayed for help and dialed while continuing to pray.

I got transferred twice and was able to talk to the person who could help me. I asked him to look at my record. He did.

"Sir," I said. "I have this new van and can't take the classes for the bus license because of the ticket on my record."

"Yeah! I see it there. So, what do you want me to do?"

"I would like you to remove the points so I can take the classes and get my bus license and drive these kids around to the activities I voluntarily provide."

"I understand your situation," he answered. "I'll take the points off for two weeks and then put them back on. Do you understand you have only two weeks to get your license?"

"Yes, I understand; thank you for your kindness. May God bless you for it."

I attended the classes, knowing it was crucial to pass the driving test on my first attempt since I only had two weeks. I completed the courses and aced the test. I thanked God for this unexpected help. Previously, I had also experienced similar support when I took my ham radio written test and the Morse code speed and accuracy test.

# CHAPTER 34

## Teen Evangelistic Mime Drama Team

One of Penny's dreams was to have an evangelistic mime drama team. She purchased several instruction books while in the United States. She told the youth group in our third church anyone could participate, but they had to be serious enough about it to show up for practice.

After many practices, our team gave its first performance at a public school. Fernanda Lopez brought her family to the event. Later, she told us, "I was the suicide girl you portrayed in the mime story. I felt God was talking to me, so I'm here to get saved." Fernanda made her decision that day.

Since most of our teens studied in the mornings, they had their afternoons free. On Tuesdays and Thursdays, we took them to two public schools. After the mime performances, we passed out Chick tracts; then we went to our house and ate the donuts I deep fried. We did this for a few years.

Penny planned for six teens to visit Uruguay to work with churches supported by Missionary Ray Pope. We also joined a week-long camp, where our teens performed dramas. During this trip, Bia, one of our cast members, received news of her father's passing. Penny and Bia returned home by bus; I stayed with the rest of the teens to finish our schedule, which included performing for a theater club and in a downtown park.

The park attracted teens who gathered with their cars, opened their hatchbacks, and tuned their radios to the same station. They leaned on their vehicles, chatted, and drank beer together.

To connect with these teens, our team split into groups and mingled among them. We asked them to turn down their radios so we could sing. Afterwards, we distributed Chick tracts. The teens responded politely.

We started our drama team again in 2022. At least five of the participants were teens whose parents were in our previous group. It was fantastic to have a second-generation drama team.

With the original team, we visited many schools. Years later, some schools contacted us, hoping we could return. Since we didn't have a teen team at that time, we gathered a few adults and taught them the skits. One participant had been on the original team.

It was because of this mime presentation that Princess Isabel School invited us to teach wrestling during school hours. This was an enormous privilege afforded only to a few people.

The only school that disliked our presentation was the one devoted to 'Our Lady Who Appeared.' According to their tradition, this saint in the Catholic Church is represented by a piece of wood found in a river by two fishermen two centuries ago. After many attempts, their empty nets finally filled with fish. The wooden statue among the fish was credited with a miracle. It is the patron saint of Brazil and the reason for a national holiday in October.

The school director handed back the Chick tract about Jesus and said, "We don't follow Jesus here: We follow 'Our Lady

Who Appeared.' Don't ever come back." And we didn't.

## *EVANGELISTIC MIME DRAMA TEAMS*

*FIRST TEAM*

*Three of these girls are now teachers in the public school. Like most of our successful outreaches, this Evangelistic Mime Drama Team was Penny's idea.*

*MORE RECENT TEAM*

PUBLIC SCHOOL USING OUR PROPERTY

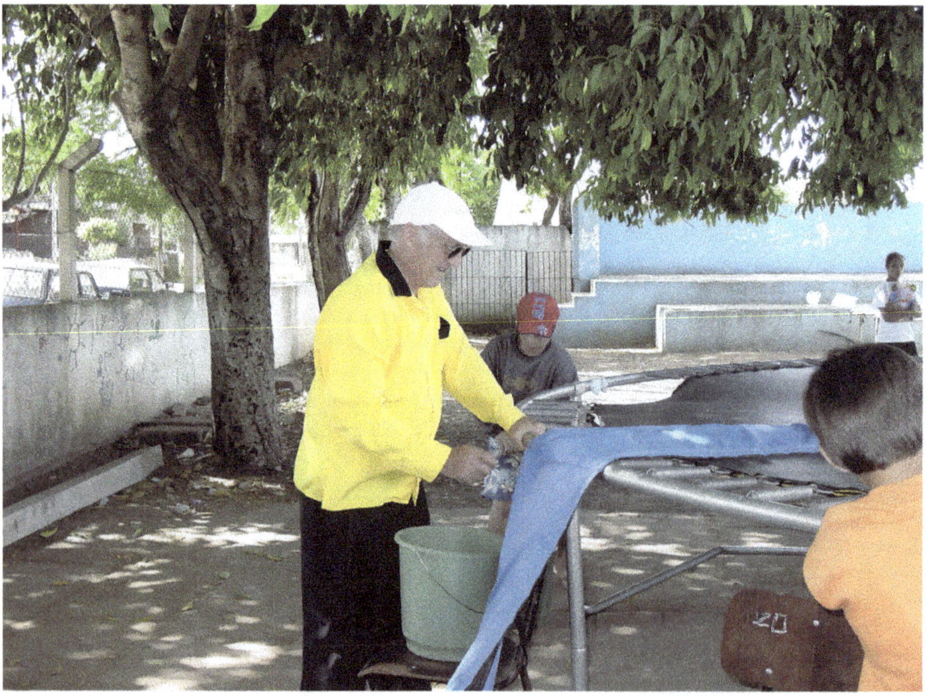

TAKING A TRAMPOLINE TO A PUBLIC SCHOOL

# CHAPTER 35

# Public School Things

We provided various activities for the public school near our house, such as drama presentations, wrestling, puppets, and trampoline sessions. The schoolchildren would walk over to use our large activity space, spending the whole day with us and even preparing a barbecue to share.

One Thanksgiving, Sandra, the school principal, called and said, "Thomas, come to the school and celebrate Thanksgiving with us." Although Thanksgiving appears on Brazil's calendar, it isn't celebrated, so I was curious about what they had planned.

When I got to the school, they sat me in a chair and called all the students to surround me. Then, Sandra said, "We're going to celebrate Thanksgiving, Pastor Thomas. Students, are you ready?"

The students replied that they were ready. Sandra then counted, "Okay—one, two, three!" and the entire school said in unison, "THANK YOU, GOD, FOR PASTOR THOMAS." I was unprepared for this surprise. My eyes filled with tears of joy.

Later, Principal Sandra approached me with a concern: "Pastor Thomas, we're having a lot of trouble with discipline at school. Can you talk to our parents about how to raise obedient children?" For comparison, such a request would be unheard of in the United States, where a public school principal asks a pastor to teach parents how to raise respectful and obedient children!

I expected around ten parents, but more than seventy arrived, filling the small room. I gave a PowerPoint presentation on raising children with love, discipline, and example. "Don't waste time telling your children not to use drugs," I told them, "if you smoke anything yourself. You must set a good example."

That one meeting led to more than forty people coming to our church. It's important to remember the idea for this meeting came from the school's principal. Also, the initial connection to the school began with donuts, an idea of Penny's.

Later, Lea Beatriz, another school principal, asked me to help with a student who was also one of my wrestlers and needed an attitude adjustment. When I arrived, he was sitting on a chair grinning, appearing quite smug.

I leaned in close and asked him, "Have you ever seen someone carrying a one-hundred-pound sack of cement on their head? I've seen some carry three sacks at once."

He replied that he had also seen men carrying three sacks of cement. Then, the boy said, "So what?"

I continued, "If you get expelled, that might be the only job available to you. So, shape up and do right, or you'll end up carrying cement for very little pay."

Lea called me again, asking, "Would you perform a marriage of a Catholic and a non-Catholic?"

"Not in our church, but what do you want?"

"I have a niece who wants to marry a man who is not a Catholic. The Catholic Church will not marry them. What can you do for her?"

I agreed to perform the wedding at a downtown hotel. During rehearsal, I asked the bride to repeat, "Until death parts us."

She asked, "Do I have to say that?"

"Aren't you going to stay married to him until you die?"

"If it works out," she adamantly said.

I was dumbfounded, having never had this problem before. "You mean you're not going to remain married to him until the end of your life?"

"If it works out," she repeated.

Her aunt yelled from the back of the room, "Say it, it's part of the ceremony." She finally agreed to say it.

Lea called me a year later, asking, "Do you baptize babies?"

"No, but what do you want?"

"My niece had twin boys, and she can't get them baptized in the Catholic Church. Can you help her?"

"I can do a child dedication ceremony in your home."

On the day of the ceremony, Penny and I visited their home. I explained to everyone, "We're not actually dedicating the boys to God today. The boys aren't aware of what's happening. Today is really about encouraging these parents to raise their boys according to God-given principles found in His Word. I'll pass this Bible around for each adult to read a relevant verse."

A year later, Lea asked me to do the dedication for another child born to the same couple.

SHANE MAKING SUSHI

# CHAPTER 36

## Food Evangelism

My son, Shane, and his wife, Erin, have shown food is a powerful tool for evangelism. Shane excels at cooking meat, while Erin also brings impressive culinary skills. Penny contributed with her talent for decorations and elegant serving—she always made sure the fork was on the left side of the plate. My specialty was making pancakes, sweet rolls, donuts, and fondue.

We started the fondue meal with a hot pot of cheese for dipping boiled potatoes, broccoli, small pieces of French bread, and tiny blocks of goiabada, a guava-based dessert.

For the next course, we used an electric skillet to serve sliced pork, chicken, and filet mignon. We seasoned the meat with only salt, including Lawry's Seasoned Salt, and provided a variety of sauces for selection.

The final course featured a pot of hot chocolate for dipping sliced bananas, pineapple, strawberries, grapes, and wafer bars. Our table seated eight people.

Nearly everyone from the church has visited our home for a meal. After that, I invited only those who were not saved. Most were happy to accept the invitation.

Workers from the telephone office came with six people. Since more expressed interest, I scheduled an additional night for their group.

While talking to the school guard during a wrestling event, I noticed two women looking my way. I asked, "Do you want to talk to the guard?"

"No, we want to talk to you."

"How can I help you?" I'm sure I had a surprised look on my face.

"We work at the clinic next door. Didn't you give us an open invitation to go to your house for dinner?"

"Yes, I did."

"Well, we want to go."

The two women came and brought others. We planned dinners for the following fifteen Mondays.

During each dinner, I shared my story of becoming a Christian—a testimony that often moves people to tears. We also provided our guests with two chapters from Jim Hazewinkel's book, *Legacy of the Mat*. These chapters discuss my experience witnessing to Olympic wrestler Chris Taylor where I explained salvation to him twice. In the same packet, guests received six different tracts by Jack Chick that presented the gospel in graphic-novel format. Finally, they got a brochure about our church's beliefs, an explanation of salvation, and a description of our church programs.

These Monday night dinners were at the heart of our approach, fostering connections and showing genuine care for our guests.

In 2023, a family of adults attended our prayer meeting after visiting our home for fondue the previous Monday. We praised God for these encouraging results.

Our church men and women also do this food evangelism once a month. They invite their unsaved friends to meet in our lovely church kitchen for barbecue, pizza, or finger food.

SOMETIMES, SHISH KABOBS WERE ON THE MENU

Penny, Núbia, and Joyce Bolhman (single missionary) started a patchwork quilt class on Wednesdays at church. We invested thousands of dollars in sewing and embroidery machines. Several ladies have been saved through this class, which includes an hour of Bible study.

Our Saturday wrestling ministry was expanded with additional afternoon youth activities at the church or at our house. I invested in two foosball games, two air hockey games, and a six-foot ball, which we pushed around on our seven-man soccer field. I usually served hot dogs, pizza, or chili. I also let them make their own sandwiches from the ingredients we provided.

*We hosted an afternoon youth activity at our house.*

*Cintia and her three girls in outfits Penny made for them.*

# CHAPTER 37

## Trickle-Down Evangelism

My evangelistic approach centers on what I call *Trickle-Down Evangelism*. Some might know this as Evangelism Explosion or Friendship Evangelism.

Trickle-down evangelism, like trickle-down economics (known for its successful, cascading, national effects), can have a profound spiritual impact on a church or missionary ministry when applied to outreach.

We saw trickle-down evangelism play out again and again in our church-planting ministry in Brazil over the last fifty years. When new converts love Jesus so much, they are willing to obey His command to go into all the world and preach the gospel, wonderful and eternal results will be coming down the pike.

The administrator of a school close to our house asked me to talk to parents about how to raise children so their students would not be such a discipline problem at school.

After having seen my PowerPoint presentation at the school, Cintia came to our house. "I used to be on the streets," she said. "I'm having a difficult time now rearing my three girls. I wanted to give them to my relatives and return to the street. After hearing what you said at the school, I decided it's my responsibility before God to keep my girls and teach them about Him."

I visited Cintia at their home. They lived in a shed no one would ever think of using, even for storing a lawnmower. The walls and floor had gaps between the slats, wide enough for snakes to slither through. The front door could be opened, but not without hitting the bunk beds! Besides the bunk beds, there was a two-burner stove and a small refrigerator.

Returning home, I told Penny we had to get this family out of that shed, because it wasn't safe. We moved her family into a house just 50 feet away and paid their rent for the next 5 years. Cintia came to our church and became a follower of Jesus Christ.

Cintia was a maid for Luciane, the wife of a lawyer. Cintia told her boss about our church. Luciane came, bringing her two sons. The boys joined our first wrestling club. Luciane told Miriam, her friend, who also came to church and brought her son.

We had a sign in front of our house which advertised the hours of our meetings. Rodrigo, a drug user, saw the sign and told his mother, Liliane, about the church. She came to church and soon accepted Christ as her Savior. Then, she brought her husband and four children to church. Two of her boys, Lucas and Douglas, joined our first wrestling team.

I went to visit Liliane at her home one day. As I was walking up her driveway, I saw a woman looking down and hurrying past me. I asked Liliane who the woman was.

"She's Carla Menezes, my neighbor and good friend," Liliane said. "She lives at the end of the road. When I told her my pastor was on his way, she said she didn't want anything to do with any pastor, so she zoomed out of here."

Carla soon visited our church, bringing her husband, Rude, and their eight children. The youngest child was Duda, who was a year old. Carla and Rude became followers of Jesus.

We were in desperate need of transportation for this large family. We asked two summer teen groups visiting us if they would help us purchase a VW bus for this family. First Baptist Church of Yuba City, California, and Calvary Baptist Church of San Francisco, California, pooled their resources and purchased the bus to provide transportation for this family of ten.

Liliane had many friends, including Rosanne, a mother of two boys. Rosanne was mad at God about something. She was walking down the road, kicking stones into the ditch. She noticed a small piece of paper. Picking it up, she read a few Bible verses, which tugged at her heart. She came to church and found peace when she opened her heart to Jesus. Her husband, Jerry, soon became a Christian. Their two boys also became a part of our first wrestling team. Some of these couples had not yet married; eventually, they got married at our home.

I put a Chick gospel tract in a mailbox. Gentil, the homeowner, called me. "I see you do home Bible studies. We want to do this."

Halfway through the study, Gentil and his wife, Patricia, decided to follow Jesus. His mother, Alba, also accepted Christ. After a while, Gentil and Patricia got married in our garage. Gentil eventually became a deacon in our church. This trickle-down evangelism brought forty people to our meetings. Our living room was filled with new converts.

I came home one day and found Penny crying. I asked her why

she was crying.

"Because I know how hard you worked to build this house and how much you love living here," Penny answered. "I'm tired of having a Sunday school class in our bedroom. I need my privacy. We're going to have to sell this house to get a church building."

Since I have always known how much Penny could handle, and when she was serious, I contacted Gentil's dad, who was also named Gentil. I knew he had many rentals. Before the sun set, we agreed to rent a piece of property fifty meters from the main thoroughfare of our city.

We hired Rude and Carla to help remodel the building that was on the new property. With our members helping on Saturdays, the remodel took us nine months. We rented the building for three years. When Gentil Sr. told us he was going to double the rent, Penny and I sold three lots we owned and purchased the property. He charged us the price for five empty lots and gave us the buildings at no additional cost.

Three simple actions—a parent meeting at a public school, a church sign, and a Chick tract—were the starting points for all this evangelism. When these initiatives were followed by friendship evangelism, the results spread in a trickle-down effect.

*Gigi (R) and Fernanda were a result of trickle-down evangelism. This started with a tract being handed out downtown, which began an avalanche of souls being saved.*

# CHAPTER 38

# Dad Ministry

My son once said, "Dad, you're a good father. That's probably because you never had one." What Shane said was true. I had thirteen stepfathers, but no real dad. One of the happiest days of my life was when the local Walmart started selling five Father's Day cards for only one dollar!

Our new Dad Ministry began to grow in our third church, inspired by the needs of children like Gigi and Fernanda. Many children, even those with fathers at home, still lacked positive role models. In Brazil, eighty percent of married men have girlfriends. This damages the family unit, causing instability for children that can have lasting effects.

I have always told our churches the best way for a man to raise his family is to love his wife as Christ loved the church and gave Himself for it. In all my formative years, I never saw this kind of love, except at my Grandpa Taylor's farm.

A dysfunctional family is a high price society pays for failing to follow the family principles found in God's Word. This works out badly for children in public schools and on the streets, where people are suffering because they are not listening to God.

In my Dad Ministry, I make children and teens feel important by hugging them and calling them Princes and Princesses. I also take them to places like *Disney on Ice*, sporting events, shopping centers, antique-car exhibitions, parks, or just to my home for a day.

When I take them to the mall to eat lunch with me at Applebee's, I also give each one twenty dollars to spend on themselves. If they have money left, they must give it back to me.

At one school's wrestling practice, I noticed a student had big holes in his shoes. I asked him what size he wore. The next day, I left him new tennis shoes at the office.

Twenty years ago, Leila, from across the street, rang our doorbell. "I hear you have a dad ministry for those who don't have a dad."

"I try to help," I answered.

She looked at her husband, Juan. "My husband didn't have a good dad. Juan is now using drugs. Can you help us?"

We got him into a drug rehab program. When he got out, Penny and I paid for a training course so he could become a security guard. Then, we found him a job and helped with their expenses until he started making money.

Leila had their first child, and Juan did well for a while—even working as an assistant pastor in São Paulo. Unfortunately, after this, he returned to using drugs. Leila had three more children.

When their youngest, Sarah, was in the first grade, Leila could no longer cope with Juan's addiction. She moved to a new place just a block away. For the last ten years, she has helped at our home. Despite the challenges, Leila has raised her children well, and we are proud of her.

My Dad Ministry extended beyond the mission field. In 1980, I took Thomas Settell, a teenager from Bryant Avenue Christian Day School, to a Minnesota Twins baseball game. Every Father's Day, he thanks me for showing kindness to a bullied kid. Gratitude like this is rare. It means a lot to me and is rewarded by the Lord.

That same year, I took another teenage boy from a supporting church in Rockford, Minnesota, to a Twins game. Whenever we visit that church, his mother thanks us.

Bryant Avenue Baptist Church also had a troubled adolescent. I taught him basic wrestling moves and offered to introduce him to Lee Kemp, a four-time world champion freestyle wrestler and car dealer near Minneapolis. The boy eagerly accepted, and I arranged the meeting.

*PUPPETEERS I TOOK TO APPLEBEES*

*These are some of the people in our church who call me "Dad," a name I am proud to be called, especially by teenagers.*

# CHAPTER 39

# Interesting People

Over the last fifty years, many interesting people have come into our lives. Some of these stories are happy, and some are sad.

**Ministry Click**

After presenting our ministry to a church, I would call the pastor within 30 days to see whether they were interested in partnering with us for church planting in Brazil.

We had been in a church where a friend of mine was the pastor. I thought monthly support was possible. "Pastor," I asked, "I was wondering if the church might consider supporting us on a monthly basis."

"Well, Tom," he answered, "to tell you the truth, your ministry just doesn't click with me."

I was using a rotary phone. My choleric personality wanted to say, "Really? Does this click with you?" as I slammed the handheld receiver into its place. Since I always try to be a Spirit-controlled Christian, I refrained from doing so. They did not support us. This pastor resigned and became the president of a mission board. I never heard from him again.

Forty years later, a friend who pastored a supporting church mentioned working with the same mission board I just mentioned above. The president of the mission board had told him I was one of the finest missionaries he'd ever known.

Imagine my surprise when I learned the name of the mission board president. Yup, the same former pastor I did not 'click with' forty years earlier. I was glad for his change of heart and for finally 'clicking' with him. Perhaps it was because we continued to serve as missionaries for many years, while others had left the field.

## Missionary Meal

Penny and I were celebrating our eighth wedding anniversary by eating at Bonanza Steak House in St. Louis, Michigan. After we prayed before our meal, a man approached us. "I saw you pray. Are you Christians?"

"We are," I answered him.

"Are you celebrating something?"

"It's our eighth anniversary," I told him.

Then, Penny added, "We're missionaries to Brazil."

"Missionaries! I love missionaries. Can I pay for your meal?" We have a custom of never turning down any gift, so we thanked him for his generosity.

## Duffel Bag Drag

Penny and I were on the sidewalk in front of the Orlando airport, with ten duffel bags to check in. A porter approached us. "I'll help you get your bags to the check-in counter."

"That's okay, I can do it," I said. "I've plenty of time."

"Please let me help you. My mother will be delighted to know I helped two missionaries today."

"Is it that obvious we are missionaries?" Penny asked.

"I can spot a missionary a mile away," he said, as he grabbed two of the duffel bags and began dragging them to the counter.

## Customs Check

We were going through customs in São Paulo, Brazil when an officer pointed to a duffel bag and asked, "What's in that bag?"

"It has olives, sunflower seeds, Lawry Seasoned Salt ..."

"Okay, what's in that other bag?"

"It has Spam," I continued, "Jif Peanut Butter ..."

"What's in that box?"

"A computer."

"You know you can't bring a computer into the country."

At that, his boss said, "Leave them alone. They're missionaries. They're probably going to use the computer for their church business."

We never mentioned being missionaries. We were left alone and allowed to pass through.

## Padded Benches

While pastoring our fourth church, I got a call. "Are you the pastor?" a nice-sounding woman asked.

"I am. What can I do for you?"

"My family is looking for a church to attend."

"How can I help you?"

"How long is your Sunday service?"

"About forty-five minutes," I replied.

"Good, because I'm tired of a preacher reading a verse then spending two hours rambling on about it. What kind of benches do you have?"

"They have a nice padding on them. They recline a bit and are very comfortable."

It was great that the family decided to come—and they stayed. Her daughter was a vital part of our drama team and one of my wrestling coaches.

## Vacation Time

In Brazil, workers receive thirty days of vacation each year, even in their first year. While we were at our first church, a man who was repairing a pipe told me, "Pastor, I'm not coming to church for the next thirty days."

"Why is that?"

"Don't I get thirty days' vacation a year?"

"From church? From God?"

"Yeah. Don't I get the vacation?"

"Well, I've never heard of a Brazilian taking a thirty-day vacation from church. It seems a bit strange to me."

I must not have been very convincing; he took his thirty days and is still taking them, I guess, because we never saw him again.

## 30,000 Volts

In our third church, just before Easter, I was preaching about Moses and the serpents of Pharaoh's wise men and sorcerers. A neighbor, who lived two houses from the church, blurted out, "Who ate those snakes?"

I told him we would talk afterwards. Following the service, he came up to me, put his mouth right up to my ear, and said, "I ate those snakes."

That surprised me. I didn't know what to say. I thought perhaps I was in the presence of God's ancient enemy. He walked out of the church.

He came back to church on Easter Sunday, with his wife holding him steady. I asked what had happened. She said he was hit with 30,000 volts at work that week. I didn't know what he might say during the service, so I said, "Try to keep him calm, if you can."

After the service ended, he stood up and announced, "There are too many churches. We need to have just one church. We need to abolish all the churches and work together." I wasn't sure whether his ideas came from God's ancient enemy or from the 30,000 volts. Either way, I was relieved when he took his ideas elsewhere.

## Jesus Talk

I was standing in front of our second church when a teenager asked me, "What does this church talk about?"

"Why are you asking?"

He pointed to the church across the street. "That church only talks about the Holy Spirit." Then, he pointed to the building on the corner. "Those people just talk about the spirits." Finally, he pointed to the church a block away. "And that church just talks about the saints. So, what do you talk about here?"

"We talk about Jesus Christ, the Son of God, who died in our place so we could have eternal life if we believe in Him."

"So, you talk about Jesus, huh?"

"That's right. We talk about Jesus."

## Head Voices

When I was helping a missionary in his church in Porto Alegre, we came out of the building after the service. A woman from across the street approached me and asked, "Are you Pastor Thomas?"

"I am. How may I help you?"

"When you turn off the lights and leave the church, someone contacts me."

"About what?" I asked.

"They say they want to talk to you."

"Who are they?"

"I don't know their name."

"Do you have a telephone?"

"No," she answered.

"Then, how do they communicate with you?"

She pointed to her head, saying, "The messages come to me in my head."

This was so strange I got goosebumps. "Well, the next time they contact you, tell them Pastor Thomas has no desire to talk to them. Can you do this favor for me?" She said she could.

We should be so joyful from God's grace that other would respond by saying "I wish I had your God."

**WARNING TO THE SQUEAMISH**

*Over the years we had uninvited visitors to our home: bugs, mice, spiders, snakes, stray cats, and other unpleasant critters.*

CLOTHES BASKET AT THE BACK OF THE HOUSE

# CHAPTER 40

## Our House Was a Zoo

In Mossoró, Penny was going to shower our young daughter. When Mom slid the shower door open and tried to push Kosy inside, the four-year-old backed up and said, "Coooobo!"

Penny thought Kosy meant the water was cold, but she hadn't turned it on yet. How could it be cold? Still, Mom tried once more to get her daughter into the shower.

Kosette repeated herself. Then, Penny remembered Kosy didn't speak English. If Kosy wasn't saying 'cold,' what was she saying? Penny thought about the sounds—Cooold, cooolbo, cobra. She realized Kosy was saying 'COBRA!' (*Portugese word for snake.*)

Penny checked the shower and found a snake scrunched up against the wall. Since I was not home, she called our sons, Tom and Shane, for help. We guessed the snake might have come inside the clothes basket we kept at the back of the house.

Another time, before our furlough, Shane and his wife, Erin, stayed in our house. They slept in the laundry room, since our second floor wasn't finished. One day, I noticed a giant toad under their high-rise bed. "Erin," I asked, "aren't you afraid of that toad?"

"Not really. Remember, I'm from Montana. If the toad is under the bed, we won't have problems with roaches or mosquitoes."

I loved this daughter-in-law and still do.

In Fortaleza, our bedroom had only one bed and nothing else. One night, while I was half asleep, I felt something run across my chest. Penny said, "Find it, or I'm not sleeping here tonight." I had an idea of what it could be.

We had some built-in closets. Inside one of the closets was a canister-type vacuum cleaner. The next day, I asked our housemaid, "Do you suppose a mouse is living in that vacuum?"

"It could go up the rubber hose," she suggested.

"Okay, when I take off the lid, the little mice might run all over the place. But, as you can see, there's nowhere for them to hide. Can you stomp them out?"

She took off her shoes and put them on her hands, like mittens. Kneeling by the vacuum cleaner, she said, "I'm ready."

When the mice came out, they headed for cover in all directions. She began decimating them. Then, her shoes flew off her hands. The maid kept swatting the little mice with her bare hands, sending them to 'The Great Cheese Picnic in the Sky'!

Later, our maid said, "I hate those loathsome critters so much, I would kill them all with my bare hands." And she did, too.

Penny and I were sitting on the bed in our home in Gravataí, when I spotted a tarantula, as big as my hand, come meandering out from under our bed—like it owned the place. "Penny, close your eyes, and I'll help you get out of the room."

"Why? What is it?"

"You don't want to know. Trust me."

"Okay." She was getting used to this.

After helping Penny out of the room, I returned, hoping the 'fright machine' hadn't crawled back under the bed. Snakes, cockroaches, ants, spiders, lizards, and rats are usually more afraid of us than we are of them. (Although, this might not be true for Penny.) Still, these critters typically run away when they see people.

Fortunately, when I returned to the bedroom, the tarantula was still moving slowly across our ceramic floor. I threw a towel over it and took the scary arachnid to the back of our acre, where it could keep killing the insects I hate, even more than I hate spiders.

Another time, a huge tarantula was 'sneaking' across our soccer field. Tarantulas are slow and easy to catch. My next move was to put it in a birdcage. A spider's favorite meal is another spider. I also put a few tiny frogs in the cage. It was fun to see the 'race for life.' When I needed to clean the cage, the tarantula apparently thought it had gained its freedom and started heading for the open door. I scooped it up in a dustpan.

The most dangerous part of a hairy tarantula is not its bite. In fact, I don't know anyone who has been bitten by one. When threatened, a tarantula can release tiny, barbed hairs that can be harmful. I found out later that day that if I hadn't been wearing glasses, those tiny, barbed hairs would have blinded me in my right eye. The experience was very painful.

There were times I was sound asleep when Penny would shake

me and yell, "Get up, there's a big spider in my office." I'd stagger into her office at 3:00 AM, so I could demonstrate my protective prowess and save this frightened damsel from her inevitable and dreadful demise.

"Where is it?" I asked.

"Right there! Can't you see it?"

I had to get down on my hands and knees and use a magnifying glass to find the dangerous spider, about half the size of a BB. "Is this the horrifying critter that scared you enough to wake me up?"

"You know how I feel about any insect. Now, you get rid of it!"

Since I've always known which side of my bread has peanut butter and jelly on it, I did as I was told, sending the almost invisible offender to 'The Great Fly Convention in the Sky.'

NÚBIA, JONAS, AND DEACON PAULO RODRIGUES

# CHAPTER 41

# Three Men Sent from God

The biblical qualifications for deacons are specified in *1 Timothy 3:8-13*. In October 1980, we left our first church without a man who met these criteria. At that time, we called Jose Bezerra to serve as the church's pastor; he later identified qualified men to serve as deacons. Similarly, in 1986, when we departed from our second church, we again lacked a qualified deacon. We then invited Ernesto Bezerra (Jose's brother) to become the pastor, and under his leadership, the church eventually installed a qualified deacon.

In my early years of church planting, many people supported me. In the last two churches, three men who became deacons stood out for their help: Paulo Rodrigues, Paulo Danni, and Antonio Pereira. Each embodied the biblical qualities expected of deacons, making a significant impact as we served together. I believe these three men were sent from God.

## PAULO RODRIGUES

At the top of a four-story building near our third church, we had painted the church's name. Paulo Rodrigues and his wife, Núbia, noticed the sign one day. Paulo remarked, "Now that we have teenagers, we need to start attending church again. Our children need Christ, and we need to walk with the Lord ourselves." Acting on this resolve, they began attending our church while Shane and Erin were covering for us during our furlough.

After our return from furlough, we visited Paulo and Núbia at their home. Soon, their teenagers, Samuel and Carolina, accepted Christ, and we baptized them. About a year later, we appointed Paulo as a deacon. Over time, he became the church's treasurer, and Núbia served as secretary.

I discovered Paulo was exceptionally good at maintaining a calm attitude during complex relationship problems. I would consult him before dealing with any church conflict. He was patient and understanding.

We were like the 'bad cop/good cop' partners. Of course, he was the good cop. He saved me a lot of grief by working with me before we tackled a problem. I so appreciated his wisdom and long suffering. These qualities helped ease the wounds we would be facing together.

Núbia became Penny's best friend. They had so much in common. They planned ladies' activities and attended patchwork conferences in Gramado, a German city 50 miles from our house.

Nathan Shirk, from Lebanon, Pennsylvania, spent several months helping with construction at our third church, and also enjoyed playing soccer in the afternoons. Six years after his initial visit, Nathan returned, met Carolina—Paulo and Núbia's daughter—and married her in our backyard six months later.

They live in Pennsylvania now, with their three children. Every time we went to a mission conference in Lebanon, Pennsylvania, we got together with them and his parents, Ken and Susie Shirk. Ken does my United States taxes every year.

Our next step in church planting was to begin a fourth church in a new location. In 2001, before leaving for furlough, we called Jose Bezerra to serve as pastor at our third church. When we started the new church in our living room in Gravataí, our deacon, Paulo Rodrigues, and his wife, Núbia, joined us in this new work.

While we were on furlough, Paulo led church services. His family, Jonas (his mother-in-law), and Bia (a teenager) supported him. When we returned, we found the church running smoothly. A few years ago, Paulo and Núbia moved to the state above us to be closer to their son, his Christian wife, and their granddaughter.

## PAULO DANNI

Sometime after 2015, when we were enjoying our fourth church, I needed the front wall of our church building replaced. The company that built our third church estimated the work at $12,000, but I only had half that. Seeking an alternative, I contacted several online construction companies.

No one answered my first two calls. On the third try, I reached Paulo Danni, who ran a two-man construction company. His estimate was half the previous bid, so I gave him the work, and he completed it with excellence.

Around that time, Paulo's wife, Zorida, saw our sign for patchwork quilting sessions at the church. She started attending the classes, where she eventually accepted Christ. Paulo followed suit soon after. I taught them my 14-chapter Bible course for new believers, and when Zorida sought baptism, Paulo did as well.

I kept finding work for him at church and at our house. Everything

Paulo did was with great contemplation and excellence. He saved me a lot of money because he knew the places to buy quality materials at the lowest price.

Paulo's mother, Maria, lived in a house on his property. She eventually got saved, but became bedridden before she could get baptized. She passed on to glory soon after her conversion.

Paulo has a gift for understanding people, which makes him invaluable for navigating personal issues within the church. I routinely seek his biblical counsel before addressing sensitive matters. He generously helps with repairs at my home, often without charge, even on Sundays. Paulo says he regards me as a father figure.

## ANTONIO PEREIRA

In 2006, Antonio (Tony) approached me to ask for permission to marry Jane da Cruz, my 'adopted' Brazilian daughter. Her father had passed away eight years earlier, and I had filled a fatherly role at her request. Tony and Jane attended his church for some time before coming to our fourth church in Gravataí.

After settling in at our Gravataí church, Tony was made a deacon within a year. Jane became the church secretary. Later, after completing Penny's teacher's course, both became Sunday school teachers.

In 2022, he became my assistant youth pastor. They have two children, Emanuel and Agatha, who was one of our female wrestlers.

I rely on Tony to lead church activities when I am unavailable and trust he will eventually succeed me as pastor. His office is already prepared, although he still needs several years of study.

Tony is the humblest Brazilian I know. He's a wonderful husband and father. The church teenagers like him. He can keep a cool head in dealing with personal problems in the church.

Tony's wife, Jane, is one of three ladies who share the duties of our monthly women's meetings. She is also a big help with the youth activities.

I believe God sent these three men—Paulo Rodrigues, Paulo Danni, and Tony—to help me. I can sometimes come across as harsh due to my choleric personality, which tends to be unsympathetic unless led by the Holy Spirit. While I always aspire to be Spirit-controlled, these men helped me achieve this in both churches. Without them, my work would have been far more difficult and less successful.

*Tony (L) and Paulo Danni (R) are such a tremendous help to me as we continue to see new people come into our church through various forms of personal evangelism.*

*Penny, with her mom, after Pillsbury Baptist Bible College graduation ceremony, where she received her diploma.*

*My favorite painting by Penny hangs in my home office.*

# CHAPTER 42

## Eulogy for Penny Sue Latham

After I accepted Christ on May 6, 1964, the first book I read was *Through Gates of Splendor*, by Elisabeth Elliot, published in 1957. The book is about five missionaries who were killed by the Aucas in Ecuador.

The second book I read was *In His Steps: What would Jesus do?*, by Charles Monroe Sheldon, published in 1896. The book emphasized making every decision based on what would Jesus do. It was the first appearance of the WWJD idea.

Reading both of these books inspired me to look for a Christian wife willing to follow Jesus anywhere. I wanted to become a missionary and commit for a lifetime.

In the summer of 1966, while working as a counselor at Camp Chetek in Wisconsin, I attended a church picnic in Waukesha. After getting my food, I noticed a young lady sitting alone and chose to join her. Next to becoming a Christian, this was the best decision I ever made.

As I sat across from this beautiful teenage girl, we started a conversation and quickly realized we knew some of the same people. I had attended Western Baptist Bible College (WBBC) in El Cerrito, California, and Penny also had connections there. She had moved from California to Wisconsin six months before I started at WBBC.

I was deeply impressed by her beauty and dedication to Jesus—she also wanted to be a missionary. Meeting her felt like finding gold. However, we faced a challenge: she planned to attend Grand Rapids School of Bible and Music in Michigan, while I would return to Pillsbury Baptist Bible College in Owatonna, Minnesota. As I watched her leave, I felt back at square one.

To my surprise, Penny showed up as a counselor at Camp Chetek. I grew even more impressed. During that time, I performed a skit about Japan, while she performed one about Brazil.

When I returned to Pillsbury, I began dating one of Penny's close friends from Wisconsin. She soon told me, "Tom, there's no future for us. You're set on being a missionary, but I won't leave the U.S. My Russian parents sacrificed too much for me to leave." Once again, my hopes for a relationship were dashed.

Penny's friend told her about our conversation. Penny told me later she immediately wanted me to ask her out, as she saw we were heading in the same direction. When I finally did, she agreed to go out with me.

After our first date, we both knew the search for a lifetime partner was over. We were married as soon as possible after the school year ended in June 1968.

I finished college and spent four years at Central Baptist Theological Seminary in Minneapolis, Minnesota. In 1973, we were appointed as missionaries to Brazil. If you knew how utterly abhorred Penny was of any crawling creature, you might find it difficult to believe she would be willing to live in a country overrun with such critters. That showed her level of dedication. She encountered tarantulas bigger than my hand, snakes in the shower, and tiny frogs that jumped on her back while she was taking a shower. Allergies were her big problem in Northeast Brazil. When they hit, she was bedridden for days.

In 1983, we moved to the southernmost state. Over our fifty years as missionaries, we started four churches: one in the Northeast and three in Southern Brazil. Through her compassion and generosity, Penny made a lasting impact on those she served. Our churches' families deeply loved her.

She had more than 40 surgeries over the last 60 years. I have had the honor of being by her side for fifty-five years. She made our family life a wonderful experience with her creativity. Back in 1979, she even planned a circus for the kids when they were bored. Our house is filled with her art projects.

While she was in the fight of her life against aggressive breast cancer, she still studied for her women's meetings at church. Penny always surprised me with her ideas, energy, and dedication. Her love for Jesus was always evident during our many years together.

Penny was so lovely in all her ways. I was the luckiest wrestler in the world to have married her. When we got married, I felt like I had won history's biggest prize.

If you knew who I was before Christ picked me up out of the ditch, you would understand how utterly elated I was to have such a lovely and wonderful person choose me. Four men had asked her to marry them, but she held out for someone who loved the Lord first and always, and was dead set on being a missionary until the end of life.

Penny dedicated our married life to supporting my happiness and well-being, her love for Jesus guiding her actions. The love we shared was a profound gift. Anyone who knew her could see the depth and authenticity of her character and our bond.

On April 30, 2023, we knew Penny had no more than a few days left. She did not want to prolong the suffering, so she took off the oxygen mask. She whispered, "Let me go to Jesus."

"Kosy is on her way," I said. "Do you want to see her one more time?" She could hardly talk. "If you want to, just nod your head," I said. She nodded.

We needed to keep the mask on so Kosy could have a final visit, too. Kosy arrived fifteen hours later and spoke to her loving mother for the last time. Everyone gathered around as Penny took her last breath on May 1, 2023. She crossed over the Jordan to be with her Savior, whom she had loved and obeyed for sixty years.

She desired to leave her missionary work and go directly to glory. She accomplished this. She now has the answers to the questions we are still struggling with.

I know we'll see her again. What a glorious reunion that will be!

*This is the final photo of Penny Sue Latham.*

# CHAPTER 43

# On Being a Missionary Kid

## by Shane Thomas Latham

What was it like to grow up as a missionary kid? More specifically, what was it like growing up in the Latham missionary family, and what core values and experiences shaped us?

My childhood in Brazil was much like Tom Sawyer's life. I had a pet monkey, a parrot, and Samson, our German Shepherd, who ate both the monkey and parrot! Our house was always full of lizards and sometimes enormous toads. I kept pigeons, hoping to train them as messenger birds, but they mostly made a mess. I even had hamsters, which I pretended were paratroopers by making them tiny parachutes.

A missionary kid's life in Brazil's northeast coast was about staying safe from snakes, tarantulas, and scorpions (and sometimes avoiding schoolwork). We chewed sugar cane, shot BB guns at each other, swam in rivers, and climbed trees for guavas and mangos the size of footballs.

Although we didn't have much by U.S. standards, with most clothes made by Mom or donated, my siblings and I felt we were the luckiest kids. Our sense of contentment and gratitude was at the heart of our childhood experience.

As a child, I often imagined our life was like the stories I loved. I searched for a hidden way into Narnia and turned our surroundings into adventures like those of the *Swiss Family Robinson* or *Tarzan*. My parents taught us the Bible and encouraged adventures, combining them in my mind with what it meant to be a missionary.

I noticed early on that our lives were constantly changing. When I was about four, someone asked for my address. I asked my dad, who joked, "Tell them you live at 4 Firestones." The joke made me laugh, even though I didn't get it at the time.

I thought moving around was normal. I remember sleeping in the station wagon, in church nurseries, in the prophet's chambers, and at camps where my dad spoke.

It was at Camp Chetek in Wisconsin, where, at the age of four, I first realized I was a sinner in need of a Savior. The revealing sin was a stolen cookie, about which I lied, denying I had stolen it. By this time, Mom and Dad had instilled in my memory hundreds of verses from the Bible, which my parents used to explain to me the good news of salvation by grace through faith alone. That gift from my parents would be enough for me to thank them throughout eternity. I will share that eternity with them, as a child who became their brother in Christ.

I remember Dad's special cereal made of toast, torn into pieces, with milk and sugar added. I remember the joy of going through missionary closets like it was Christmas, choosing coloring books and crayons, while Dad selected tools, and Mom picked out towels and bed sheets to take to Brazil.

Up until I was twelve, family nights, meals, and stories filled my memories. My parents shaped a loving, faith-filled home. As first-generation Christians, they were building a foundation rooted in sacrifice and perseverance, qualities that defined our family journey.

I have apologized and received forgiveness for my rebellious teen years, which brought great strain to the life they were working so hard to provide. They never gave up on me.

At fourteen, while sneaking back into the house from another episode of secretive, destructive behavior, I listened at their door and heard them praying for wisdom to reach my heart.

God lifted me out of that difficult period. Ten years later, after a lot of worry, effort, and tears from my parents, Mom flew from Brazil to Montana for my minister ordination and gave me an old page from my preteen Bible. I still have it. Alongside my father's notes, such as 'Direction, not Distance, Determines Destiny,' were my own childhood writings, in which I committed to becoming a missionary. Mom kept that page, praying, and believing God would reach me. He did.

The Latham 'creed,' which my wife and I have passed to our children, is: *All I am, all I have—serving Jesus for the time that's left.* This guiding mission continues to shape our lives—service and devotion remain our core.

Looking back, the most significant result of my upbringing is that, through God's grace, my children have chosen the same spiritual path. They serve Him with the same commitment their grandparents passed down. Today, my wife and I support and help Dad, carrying on the family tradition of faith and unity.

As Forrest Gump would say, "That's all I have to say about that."

*My son, Shane, and his wife, Erin, live upstairs in my house.*
*It's a tremendous blessing to have them so close.*
*(Also, I get a lot of free meals.)*

*Thomas was the clown and magician in our backyard*
*circus.*

# CHAPTER 44

# Another Missionary Kid's Life

## by Tom Latham Jr.

I spent my childhood in Northeast Brazil, where tropical ice cream came in passion fruit and pineapple flavors. My first challenge was learning Portuguese. Once my parents enrolled me in a Brazilian public school, I picked it up quickly. By age 11, I was in the sixth grade and began attending a boarding school. Looking back, it often feels like I lived ten lifetimes in one: as a missionary kid, I had already traveled coast-to-coast in the U.S. and started living abroad by the age of six.

While living in Mossoró from 1976 to 1980, I remember when a circus visited our town. I saw elephants bathing in the river between acts, while nearby, women washed clothes along the riverbank. Children played in the water, and older kids balanced water cans on their heads as they walked home.

My mom was an artist and inspired us to put on our own backyard circus. We gathered friends to help with magic and clown acts, and sold tickets for the event. The backyard circus was a huge success, and I took on the role of the magician. I still keep in touch with some of those friends today.

As a teenager in Southern Brazil, I learned to play the guitar, improved my harmonica skills, and started writing music, poetry, and lyrics. By then, I had spent nearly eight formative years in

Brazil, shaping both Brazilian and American expat identities. Today, I appreciate the Brazilian outlook on life: if you have good health and the essentials for your family, you have much to celebrate. My American roots, meanwhile, encouraged patriotism and hard work.

I left Brazil as a teenager and received a missionary-kid scholarship for college. Adjusting to life in the U.S. was difficult after missing out on pop culture trends and not knowing how to fit in. Over time, my mix of Brazilian and American cultures became a strength, making me adaptable and resilient. This flexibility helped in the U.S. Army, and the challenges of my youth made military deployments easier to manage.

Now retired, I spend my time writing and traveling. My missionary-kid upbringing and military background fostered a nomadic spirit, leaving me ready for new adventures. To me, something as simple as black coffee on a floating house on the Amazon River or a nap in a hammock feels luxurious.

From 2002 to 2008, I served as a missionary in the Amazon while raising four kids. One of my children later married a Brazilian, bringing the missionary kid experience full circle for our family. Recently, I moved back to Brazil to be near my international family. In April 2024, my journey as an MK (Missionary Kid) reached another milestone when I married a Brazilian woman I met through my dad's wrestling ministry.

I'm a missionary kid, a missionary, and the father of missionary kids.

*My son, Thomas (Tom Jr.), with his wife, Carine.*

> "I have no greater joy than to hear that my children walk in truth."
>
> 3 John 1:4

> *"Train up a child in the way he should go: and when he is old, he will not depart from it."*
>
> *Proverbs 22:6*

KOSY'S AND MIKE'S FURRY FAMILY
CODY (TERRIER) AND OSA (AUSTRALIAN SHEPHERD)

# CHAPTER 45

# A Daughter's Perspective

## by Kosette "Kosy" Latham Cambre

Growing up in Brazil as a missionary kid, my childhood was shaped by ministry long before I realized how unique that was. Brazil was more than just where my father worked; it was home. Portuguese filled our house, and it was the first language I spoke.

Daily life moved at a different pace than what I later found in the States, and faith was part of everyday moments, not just something for Sundays. I learned to observe, adapt, and listen by watching my parents live out their calling with consistency and humility. For me, open doors, shared meals, and prayers in more than one language were simply a part of life.

As a child, I didn't always understand what it meant to grow up in another culture, but it shaped who I became. Living between two worlds taught me to be flexible, empathetic, and to respect cultures different from my own. Brazil showed me the gospel isn't limited to one language or lifestyle, and my father's work taught me faith is strongest when lived out every day, not just spoken about.

Now, I see my upbringing was less about where I lived and more about the lessons I learned from my parents' service, sacrifice, and a deep love for God and the people of Brazil.

Once, I owned my own salon business. I also worked in medical care, home health, hospice, and as a waitress. Now we are full-time RVers. In the summer, we are based in Colorado because I am a Camp Host, and Michael works remotely as an Executive General Adjuster. In the wintertime, we travel the country.

*My daughter, Kosy, with her husband, Mike (Cambre).*

# More Pictures

*Quentin and Lana Freeburg hosted Shane for a year.*

*Kosy (far right) stayed with the Dennis Sleen family for a year. Thomas (center back) joined her for a visit.*

*Kosy with our dog Samson. Samson bit into a toad and quickly spit it out. The amphibian excreted juice that gave the dog a horrible taste in its mouth.*

*Shane made popcorn, and I made churros (fried pastry dough dipped in sugar) for a church event.*

*I'm modeling an authentic Brazilian Gaucho outfit.*

*I'm with Penny during our 50th wedding anniversary celebration in 2018.*

**THE LATHAM FAMILY - 2023**

BACK: TOM JR., KOSY, AND SHANE
FRONT: PENNY AND TOM

# Author Biography
—
# Dr. Tom Latham

GENERAL QUARTERS DRILL

Tom Latham became a Christian while serving in the U.S. Navy, where he began holding *Protestant Divine Services* whenever his ship was at sea. After completing his naval service, he spent the next four years at bible college to further his spiritual journey. He achieved a significant milestone in his studies by earning a

Doctor of Ministry (DMin) degree from Luther Rice Seminary.

Tom met Penny Stimpson, and together they began a mission to serve God in Brazil. Their family grew to include three children, six grandchildren, and ten great-grandchildren.

PREACHING AS A GAUCHO

Although Penny was promoted to glory, Tom continues to serve Christ in Brazil.



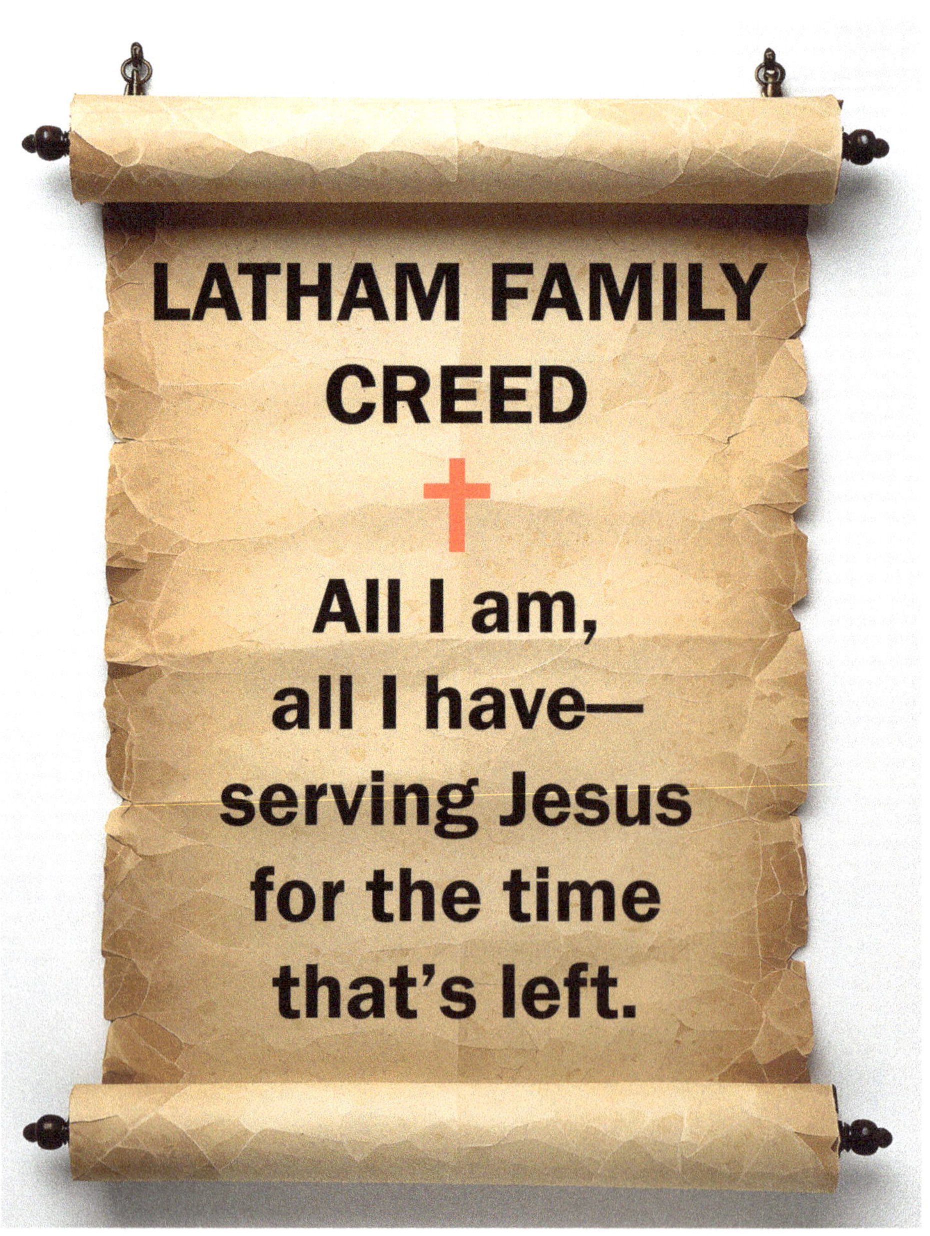

# Acknowledgments and Thanks

I acknowledge Jesus Christ, my Savior. Without His guidance and grace lifting me from a spiritual ditch, this book would not exist. I owe Him more than I can ever repay.

I thank my three children, Thomas, Shane, and Kosette, for making life an adventure as we faced the challenges and joys of the mission field in Brazil. Their companionship gave us more experiences than those in my more than 70 manuscripts, which may eventually become published books.

I thank Bob Cundiff, PhD, for his professional editorial and proofreading assistance. Bob resides in Clearwater, Florida. He teaches communication at St. Petersburg College and has edited or co-edited three other books. Bob is a published and produced playwright, a voiceover artist, and a member of The Gideons International.

I thank June May Harness for her many hours of proofreading my writing. June resides in New Port Richey, Florida. She worked with Bob Cundiff on the book *Legacy of the Mat*, by Jim Hazewinkel. She is a retired schoolteacher and the widow of Rev. Clytee Harness. She has two children and seven grandchildren.

I also thank Dave Carlson, owner of DynoTech Publishing, a proper 'jack of all trades' and 'master of many,' for his invaluable contribution to the publishing process. His tremendous efforts far exceeded what I could have accomplished alone, and I am deeply grateful. Dave, a brother wrestler who resides in Colorado Springs, Colorado, stays busy during retirement with consulting projects related to computer technology, computer-aided illustration, book editing, and publishing.

> *"Giving thanks always for all things unto God and the Father in the name of our Lord Jesus Christ"*
>
> *Ephesians 5:20*

## More Books by Dr. Tom Latham
### SHANE WOODS SERIES

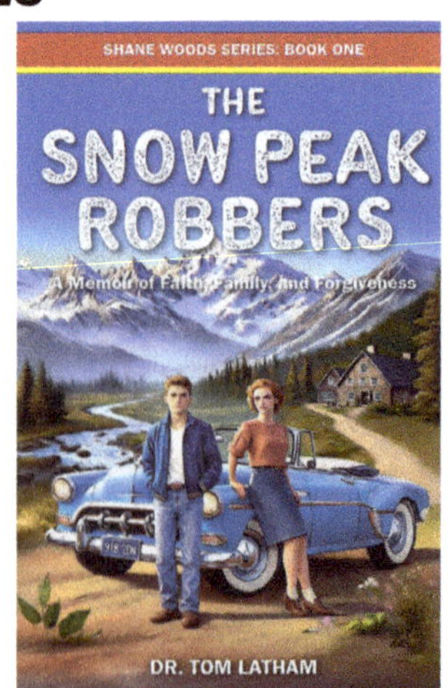


Book One:    *The Snow Peak Robbers*
             ISBN 978-1-885708-51-9

Book Two:    *The Strawberry Fair*
             ISBN 978-1-885708-52-6

Book Three: *The Buzzard Butte Poachers*
             ISBN 978-1-885708-53-3

Book Four:   *The Eastern Rodeo*
             ISBN 978-1-885708-54-0

*Future books in the series will depend on reader interest. More book sales may motivate me to publish more of my existing 15+ manuscripts in this series.*

*My first wrestling team is wearing homemade singlets with Minnesota Gophers colors.*

PASTOR ERNESTO
AND LUZIA
IN FRONT OF THE
PARSONAGE

RUDE & CARLA WITH FAMILY AND VW BUS WE BOUGHT

www.ingramcontent.com/pod-product-compliance
Lightning Source LLC
Chambersburg PA
CBHW050025040726
47599CB00015B/1541